# Dreamweaver CS3: Basic

## Student Manual

ACE Edition

# Dreamweaver CS3: Basic

| | |
|---|---|
| **President & Chief Executive Officer:** | Michael Springer |
| **Vice President, Product Development:** | Adam A. Wilcox |
| **Vice President, Operations:** | Josh Pincus |
| **Director of Publishing Systems Development:** | Dan Quackenbush |
| **Writer:** | Steve English |
| **Developmental Editor:** | Brandon Heffernan |
| **Series Designer:** | Adam A. Wilcox |

## Trademarks

ILT Series is a trademark of Axzo Press.

Some of the product names and company names used in this book have been used for identification purposes only and may be trademarks or registered trademarks of their respective manufacturers and sellers.

## Disclaimers

We reserve the right to revise this publication and make changes from time to time in its content without notice.

The Adobe Approved Certification Courseware logo is either a registered trademark or trademark of Adobe Systems Incorporated in the United States and/or other countries. The Adobe Approved Certification Courseware logo is a proprietary trademark of Adobe. All rights reserved.

The ILT Series is independent from ProCert Labs, LLC and Adobe Systems Incorporated, and are not affiliated with ProCert Labs and Adobe in any manner. This publication may assist students to prepare for an Adobe Certified Expert exam, however, neither ProCert Labs nor Adobe warrant that use of this material will ensure success in connection with any exam.

Student Manual
ISBN-10: 1-4260-9718-2
ISBN-13: 978-1-4260-9718-8

Student Manual with data CD
ISBN-10: 1-4260-9720-4
ISBN-13: 978-1-4260-9720-1

Printed in the United States of America

1 2 3 4 5 6 7 8 9 10 GL 10 09 08

# Contents

# Introduction

After reading this introduction, you'll know how to:

**A** Use ILT Series manuals in general.

**B** Use prerequisites, a target student description, course objectives, and a skills inventory to properly set your expectations for the course.

**C** Re-key this course after class.

# Topic A:  About the manual

### ILT Series philosophy

Our manuals facilitate your learning by providing structured interaction with the software itself. While we provide text to explain difficult concepts, the hands-on activities are the focus of our courses. By paying close attention as your instructor leads you through these activities, you'll learn the skills and concepts effectively.

We believe strongly in the instructor-led class. During class, focus on your instructor. Our manuals are designed and written to facilitate your interaction with your instructor and not to call attention to manuals themselves.

We believe in the basic approach of setting expectations, delivering instruction, and providing summary and review afterwards. For this reason, lessons begin with objectives and end with summaries. We also provide overall course objectives and a course summary to provide both an introduction to and closure on the entire course.

### Manual components

The manuals contain these major components:

- Table of contents
- Introduction
- Units
- Appendix
- Course summary
- Quick reference
- Glossary
- Index

Each element is described below.

#### Table of contents

The table of contents acts as a learning roadmap.

#### Introduction

The introduction contains information about our training philosophy and our manual components, features, and conventions. It contains target student, prerequisite, objective, and setup information for the specific course.

#### Units

Units are the largest structural component of the course content. A unit begins with a title page that lists objectives for each major subdivision, or topic, within the unit. Within each topic, conceptual and explanatory information alternates with hands-on activities. Units conclude with a summary comprising one paragraph for each topic, and an independent practice activity that gives you an opportunity to practice the skills you've learned.

The conceptual information takes the form of text paragraphs, exhibits, lists, and tables. The activities are structured in two columns, one telling you what to do, the other providing explanations, descriptions, and graphics.

### Appendix

The appendix for this course lists the Adobe Certified Expert (ACE) exam objectives for Dreamweaver CS3, along with references to corresponding coverage in ILT Series courseware.

### Course summary

This section provides a text summary of the entire course. It's useful for providing closure at the end of the course. The course summary also indicates the next course in this series, if there is one, and lists additional resources you might find useful as you continue to learn about the software.

### Quick reference

The quick reference is an at-a-glance job aid summarizing some of the more common features of the software.

### Glossary

The glossary provides definitions for all of the key terms used in this course.

### Index

The index at the end of this manual makes it easy for you to find information about a particular software component, feature, or concept.

## Manual conventions

We've tried to keep the number of elements and the types of formatting to a minimum in the manuals. This approach aids in clarity and makes the manuals more elegant looking. But there are some conventions and icons you should know about.

| Item | Description |
|---|---|
| *Italic text* | In conceptual text, indicates a new term or feature. |
| **Bold text** | In unit summaries, indicates a key term or concept. In an independent practice activity, indicates an explicit item that you select, choose, or type. |
| `Code font` | Indicates code or syntax. |
| `Longer strings of ▶ code will look ▶ like this.` | In the hands-on activities, any code that's too long to fit on a single line is divided into segments by one or more continuation characters (▶). This code should be entered as a continuous string of text. |
| Select **bold item** | In the left column of hands-on activities, bold sans-serif text indicates an explicit item that you select, choose, or type. |
| Keycaps like ↵ ENTER | Indicate a key on the keyboard you must press. |

## Hands-on activities

The hands-on activities are the most important parts of our manuals. They're divided into two primary columns. The "Here's how" column gives short instructions to you about what to do. The "Here's why" column provides explanations, graphics, and clarifications. Here's a sample:

*Do it!*

### A-1: Creating a commission formula

| Here's how | Here's why |
|---|---|
| 1 Open Sales | This is an oversimplified sales compensation worksheet. It shows sales totals, commissions, and incentives for five sales reps. |
| 2 Observe the contents of cell F4 | F4 ▼ ＝ =E4*C_Rate<br><br>The commission rate formulas use the name "C_Rate" instead of a value for the commission rate. |

For these activities, we've provided a collection of data files designed to help you learn each skill in a real-world business context. As you work through the activities, you modify and update these files. Of course, you might make a mistake and therefore want to re-key the activity starting from scratch. To make it easy to start over, you rename each data file at the end of the first activity in which the file is modified. Our convention for renaming files is to add the word "My" to the beginning of the file name. In the above activity, for example, a file called "Sales" is being used for the first time. At the end of this activity, you would save the file as "My sales," thus leaving the "Sales" file unchanged. If you make a mistake, you can start over using the original "Sales" file.

In some activities, however, it might not be practical to rename the data file. If you want to retry one of these activities, ask your instructor for a fresh copy of the original data file.

# Topic B:  Setting your expectations

Properly setting your expectations is essential to your success. This topic will help you do that by providing:

- Prerequisites for this course
- A description of the target student
- A list of the objectives for the course
- A skills assessment for the course

## Course prerequisites

Before taking this course, you should be familiar with personal computers and the use of a keyboard and a mouse. Furthermore, this course assumes that you've completed the following courses or have equivalent experience:

- *Windows XP: Basic,* or *Windows Vista: Basic*

## Target student

This course will benefit students who want to learn to use Dreamweaver CS3 to create and modify Web sites. You'll learn how to format text, apply styles, create tables, manage images and links, manage Web site files, and publish a site. You should be comfortable using a PC and have experience with Microsoft Windows XP or Vista. You should have little or no experience with Dreamweaver.

### Adobe ACE certification

This course is designed to help you pass the Adobe Certified Expert (ACE) exam for Dreamweaver CS3. For complete certification training, you should complete this course and *Dreamweaver CS3: Advanced, ACE Edition*.

## Course objectives

These overall course objectives will give you an idea about what to expect from the course. It's also possible that they'll help you see that this course isn't the right one for you. If you think you either lack the prerequisite knowledge or already know most of the subject matter to be covered, you should let your instructor know that you think you're misplaced in the class.

**Note:** In addition the general objectives listed below, specific ACE exam objectives are listed at the beginning of each topic (where applicable). For a complete mapping of ACE objectives to ILT Series content, see Appendix A.

After completing this course, you'll know how to:

- Discuss basic Internet and HTML concepts, identify the components of the Dreamweaver CS3 workspace, edit and format text on an existing page, insert images, preview pages in a browser, identify basic HTML tags, and perform basic tasks in Code view.

- Plan and define a Web site, work with the Files panel and the Assets panel, create a Web page, import text from external files, and set page properties.

- Convert line breaks to paragraph breaks, insert special characters, define a basic page structure, create and modify lists, create CSS style sheets, apply styles to text, and create class styles and pseudo-element styles.

- Create tables and nested tables, format rows and cells, merge cells, add rows and columns to tables, set fixed and variable widths for tables and columns, change cell borders and padding, and create a layout table to arrange page content.

- Choose appropriate image formats, insert images, modify image properties, insert and modify background images, and write effective alternate text.

- Create links to other pages and resources, create named anchors and link to them, create e-mail links, create an image map, and apply CSS styles to link states.

- Work with Map view, check file sizes and download times, check for broken links and orphaned files, cloak files, validate code, connect to a Web server with a secure FTP connection, and upload and update a Web site.

## Skills inventory

Use the following form to gauge your skill level entering the class. For each skill listed, rate your familiarity from 1 to 5, with five being the most familiar. *This isn't a test.* Rather, it's intended to provide you with an idea of where you're starting from at the beginning of class. If you're wholly unfamiliar with all the skills, you might not be ready for the class. If you think you already understand all of the skills, you might need to move on to the next course in the series. In either case, you should let your instructor know as soon as possible.

| Skill | 1 | 2 | 3 | 4 | 5 |
|---|---|---|---|---|---|
| Identifying components of the Dreamweaver workspace | | | | | |
| Inserting, editing, and formatting text | | | | | |
| Inserting images | | | | | |
| Previewing pages in a browser | | | | | |
| Working in Code view | | | | | |
| Defining a site | | | | | |
| Creating and titling Web pages | | | | | |
| Importing text | | | | | |
| Setting page properties | | | | | |
| Changing line breaks to paragraph breaks | | | | | |
| Inserting special characters and spaces | | | | | |
| Applying structural tags | | | | | |
| Creating and formatting lists | | | | | |
| Creating and attaching external style sheets | | | | | |
| Creating element styles and class styles | | | | | |
| Creating pseudo-element styles | | | | | |
| Creating tables and nested tables | | | | | |
| Adding and formatting table rows and columns | | | | | |
| Creating and formatting a layout table | | | | | |
| Modifying image properties | | | | | |
| Adding background images | | | | | |

| Skill | 1 | 2 | 3 | 4 | 5 |
|---|---|---|---|---|---|
| Creating links | | | | | |
| Creating and linking to named anchors | | | | | |
| Creating external and e-mail links | | | | | |
| Creating an image map | | | | | |
| Applying link styles | | | | | |
| Working with Map view | | | | | |
| Checking page size and download time | | | | | |
| Checking for broken links and orphaned files | | | | | |
| Cloaking files | | | | | |
| Validating code | | | | | |
| Connecting to a server | | | | | |
| Uploading a Web site | | | | | |

# Topic C:    Re-keying the course

If you have the proper hardware and software, you can re-key this course after class. This section explains what you'll need in order to do so and how to do it.

## Hardware requirements

Your personal computer should have:

- A keyboard and a mouse
- Intel® Pentium® 4 or equivalent processor
- 512 MB RAM
- 1 GB of hard-disk space
- A DVD-ROM drive for installation
- An XGA monitor with 1024×768 resolution and 24-bit color support

## Software requirements

You also need the following software:

- Microsoft® Windows® XP with Service Pack 2 or Windows Vista™ Home Premium, Business, Ultimate, or Enterprise (certified for 32-bit editions); updated with the most recent service packs
- Dreamweaver CS3
- Microsoft Outlook, Thunderbird, or another e-mail client (required to complete Activity A-3 in the "Links" unit)
- Microsoft Word 2000, XP, 2003, or 2007 (Required to complete Activity B-2 in the "Web pages and sites" unit)

## Network requirements

The following network components and connectivity are also required for rekeying this course:

- Internet access, for the following purposes:
  - Updating the Windows operating system at update.microsoft.com.
  - Completing Activity A-3 in the "Links" unit
  - Downloading the Student Data files (if necessary)

## Setup instructions to re-key the course

Before you re-key the course, you need to perform the following steps.

1 Install Windows XP Professional on an NTFS partition according to the software manufacturer's instructions.

   **Note:** You can also use Windows Vista, although the screen shots in this course were taken in Windows XP, so students' screens might look somewhat different.

2 If the operating system is Windows XP, then launch the Control Panel, open the Display Properties dialog box and apply the following settings:

   • Theme—Windows XP

   • Screen resolution—1024 by 768 pixels

   • Color quality—High (24 bit) or higher

3 If Windows was already loaded on this PC, verify that Internet Explorer is the default Web browser. (If you installed Windows yourself, skip this step.)

   a Click Start, All Programs, Internet Explorer.

   b Choose Tools, Internet Options.

   c Check "Internet Explorer should check to see whether it is the default browser."

   d Click OK to close the Internet Options dialog box.

   e Close and re-open Internet Explorer.

   f If a prompt appears, asking you to make Internet Explorer your default browser, click Yes.

   g Close Internet Explorer.

4 Connect to the Internet.

5 Open Internet Explorer and navigate to update.microsoft.com. Update the operating system with the latest critical updates and service packs.

6 Install Dreamweaver CS3 according to the software manufacturer's instructions.

7 Install Microsoft Outlook, Thunderbird, or any similar e-mail application. Accept all defaults during installation. (This action is required to complete Activity A-3 in the "Links" unit.)

8 Install Microsoft Word 2000, XP, 2003, or 2007 according to the software manufacturer's instructions. Accept all defaults during installation. (This is required to complete Activity B-2 in the "Web pages and sites" unit.)

9 If necessary, reset any defaults that you've changed. If you don't wish to reset the defaults, you can still re-key the course, but some activities might not work exactly as documented.

10 Adjust the computer's display settings as follows:

   a Right-click the desktop and choose Properties to open the Display Properties dialog box.

   b On the Settings tab, change the Color quality to 16 bit or higher and the Screen resolution to 1024 by 768 pixels. (If your monitor is small, consider using a higher screen resolution, if possible.)

   c On the Appearance tab, set Windows and buttons to Windows XP style.

   d Click OK. If you're prompted to accept the new settings, click OK and click Yes. Then, if necessary, close the Display Properties dialog box.

11 Change Internet properties as follows:

    a  Start Internet Explorer. Choose Tools, Internet Options.

    b  On the General tab, click Use Blank and click Apply.

    c  On the Advanced tab, under Security, check "Allow active content to run in files on My Computer" and click Apply. (This option appears only if you updated Windows XP with Service Pack 2.)

    d  Close the Internet Options dialog box, and close Internet Explorer.

12 If necessary, create an e-mail account in your e-mail client. (You don't actually send or receive messages in this course, so a fully functional e-mail account isn't needed.) Without an e-mail client, you can't complete activity A-3 in the Links unit.

13 Display file extensions.

    a  Start Windows Explorer.

    b  Choose Tools, Folder Options and select the View tab.

    c  Clear the check box for Hide extensions for known file types.

    d  Close Windows Explorer.

14 Create a folder called Student Data at the root of the hard drive (C:\).

15 Download the Student Data files for the course. (If you don't have an Internet connection, you can ask your instructor for a copy of the data files on a disk.)

    a  Connect to www.axzopress.com.

    b  Under Downloads, click Instructor-Led Training.

    c  Browse the subject categories to locate your course. Then click the course title to display a list of available downloads. (You can also access these downloads through our Catalog listings.)

    d  Click the link(s) for downloading the Student Data files, and follow the instructions that appear on your screen.

16 Copy the data files to the Student Data folder.

## CertBlaster exam preparation for ACE certification

CertBlaster pre- and post-assessment software is available for this course. To download and install this free software, complete the following steps:

1 Go to www.axzopress.com.

2 Under Downloads, click CertBlaster.

3 Click the link for Dreamweaver CS3.

4 Save the .EXE file to a folder on your hard drive. (**Note**: If you skip this step, the CertBlaster software will not install correctly.)

5 Click Start and choose Run.

6 Click Browse and then navigate to the folder that contains the .EXE file.

7 Select the .EXE file and click Open.

8 Click OK and follow the on-screen instructions. When prompted for the password, enter **c_dwCS3**.

# Unit 1

## Getting started

**Unit time: 60 minutes**

Complete this unit, and you'll know how to:

**A** Discuss basic Internet, HTML, and XHTML concepts.

**B** Identify the components of the Dreamweaver CS3 workspace.

**C** Edit and format text on an existing Web page, insert images, and preview a page in a browser.

**D** View the HTML code of a page, identify fundamental HTML tags, and perform basic tasks in Code view.

# Topic A:  Internet basics

*Explanation*

Before you start using Dreamweaver to design and create Web sites, you should first understand the basics of the Internet, the Web, and HTML.

## The Internet and the Web

The *Internet* is a vast array of networks that belong to universities, businesses, organizations, governments, and individuals all over the world. The World Wide Web, or simply the *Web*, is one of many services of the Internet. Other Internet services include e-mail, File Transfer Protocol (FTP), and instant messaging.

To view Web pages and other content, you need a Web browser, such as Internet Explorer, Firefox, or Safari. Web content typically includes text, images, and multimedia files. Each page or resource has a unique address known as a *Uniform Resource Locater* (URL).

A *Web site* is a collection of linked pages. The top-level page is commonly called the *home page*. A home page typically provides hyperlinks to navigate to other pages within the site or to external pages. A *hyperlink*, or *link* for short, is text or an image that, when clicked, takes the user to another page, another place on the current page, or another Web site.

## HTML

*Hypertext Markup Language,* or *HTML,* is a standard markup language on the Web. HTML enables you to structure and present your Web site's content. An HTML document is a plain text file that contains HTML code, along with the content for a Web page. Exhibit 1-1 shows an example of a simple HTML document. You can create an HTML document by using any text editor, such as Notepad (Windows) or TextEdit (Mac). HTML documents have either an .htm or .html file extension.

HTML code encloses your text content and defines the basic structure of a Web page. A Web page can contain links, references to images, multimedia files, and other elements. When a browser opens a Web page, the text typically loads quickly, while images and embedded media files might take longer.

## XHTML

The *Extensible Hypertext Markup Language,* or XHTML, is a stricter version of HTML. For years, browser makers introduced proprietary tags and attributes in an effort to give Web designers more control over the look and feel of their Web pages. Unfortunately, most of these elements and attributes served only to make Web page code bloated, cluttered, and semantically meaningless. This development made it more time-consuming to author Web pages and far more difficult and time-consuming to update and maintain them. XHTML doesn't allow proprietary tags and attributes, but it does allow for cleaner, more efficient code. By default, Dreamweaver CS3 builds Web pages with XHTML code.

```
<!DOCTYPE html PUBLIC "-//W3C//DTD XHTML 1.0 Transitional//EN" "http://
<html xmlns="http://www.w3.org/1999/xhtml">
<head>
<meta http-equiv="Content-Type" content="text/html; charset=utf-8" />
<title>Chili Facts</title>
</head>

<body>
<h1>Chilis</h1>
<p>Chilis add zest to many recipes. </p>
<img src="chilis.jpg" alt="Chilis" />
</body>
</html>
```

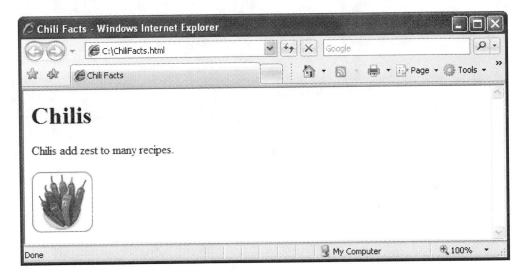

*Exhibit 1-1: A simple Web page shown as XHTML code and in a browser*

*Do it!*     **A-1: Discussing the Web, HTML, and XHTML**

### Questions and answers

1 What's the difference between the Internet and the World Wide Web?

2 What other Internet services are there?

3 What's a Web page?

4 What's a Web site?

5 What's a Web browser?

6 What's HTML?

7 What's XHTML?

# Topic B:  The Dreamweaver workspace

This topic covers the following Adobe ACE exam objective for Dreamweaver CS3.

| # | Objective |
|---|-----------|
| **3.1** | List and describe how to navigate the Dreamweaver UI. |

### Web authoring in Dreamweaver CS3

*Explanation*

Dreamweaver CS3 is Web authoring software that helps you design and create Web pages and sites. When you create or change a page in the Dreamweaver workspace, Dreamweaver automatically generates the required XHTML, CSS, or scripting code for the page. You can also write or edit code yourself. Before creating Web sites, you should become familiar with the Dreamweaver workspace.

### Opening files

To open a file in Dreamweaver:

1  Start Dreamweaver CS3. The Workspace Setup dialog box appears.
2  Verify that Designer is selected and click OK. The welcome screen appears, as shown in Exhibit 1-2.
3  (Optional) Check Don't show again, and click OK.
4  Choose File, Open and browse to locate the file you want to open. Select the file and click Open, or double-click the file.

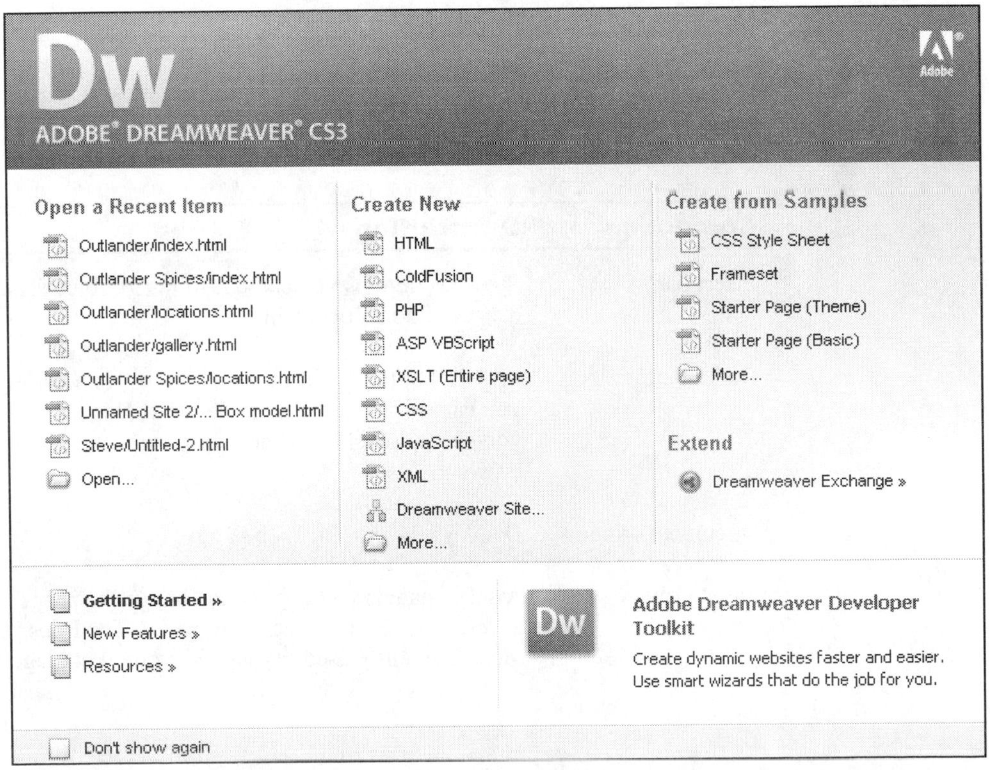

*Exhibit 1-2: The welcome screen*

## Interface components

As shown in Exhibit 1-3, the Dreamweaver default interface elements include the Insert bar, the document toolbar, the document window, the panel groups, the zoom tools, and the property inspector.

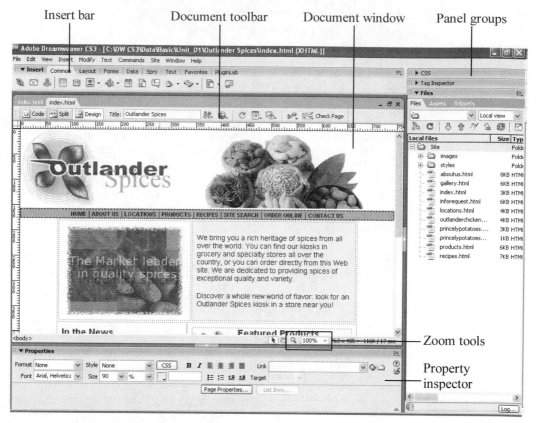

*Exhibit 1-3: The Dreamweaver CS3 interface*

The following table describes the components of the Dreamweaver interface.

| Component | Description |
|---|---|
| Insert bar | Provides buttons you can use to insert objects, such as images, tables, and div tags into a document. |
| Document toolbar | Provides buttons you can use to perform a variety of tasks. For example, you can switch between Code view, Design view, and Split view, and you can upload files, check for errors, and preview a page in a Web browser. |
| Document window | Displays the current Web page. |
| Panel groups | A set of panels you can use to change the properties of a Web page. To access a panel, click the panel name. The Files panel group is often the most frequently used; it displays your Web pages and site folders. |

| Component | Description |
| --- | --- |
| Zoom tools | (The Zoom tool and the Zoom list.) Provide ways to zoom in and out of document pages. For example, using the Zoom tool, click anywhere on the page to zoom in. To zoom out, press and hold the Alt key, and then click on the page. You can also drag a marquee around a specific area of a page to zoom in on that area, or you can select a magnification from the Zoom list. |
| Property inspector | A context-sensitive tool that displays the properties of the selected object. You can click the expander arrow in the lower-right corner of the Property inspector to display more options. |

**Visual aids**

*Visual aids* are page icons, symbols, or borders that are visible only within Dreamweaver. You can turn individual visual aids on and off to make it easier to work with a page. To set your visual aids, choose a visual aid from the Visual Aid list in the document toolbar, as shown in Exhibit 1-4. To toggle all visual aids on or off, press Ctrl+Shift+I.

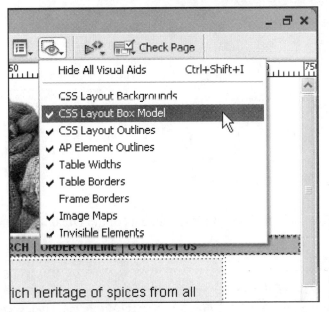

*Exhibit 1-4: The Visual Aids list in the document toolbar*

**Tabbed documents**

You can display multiple documents in a window by using tabs. You can also display documents as floating documents, in which case each document appears in its own window. To open each tabbed document in a floating window, choose Windows, Cascade. To display floating windows in a tabbed format, click the Maximize button in the upper-right corner of any floating window.

*Do it!*

## B-1: Identifying Dreamweaver interface components

| Here's how | Here's why |
|---|---|
| 1 Choose **Start**, **All Programs**, **Adobe Dreamweaver CS3** | To start Dreamweaver CS3. If the Default Editor dialog box appears, click OK. |
| 2 At the bottom of the welcome screen, check **Don't show again** | (To prevent the welcome screen from appearing whenever Dreamweaver CS3 starts.) A dialog box appears, indicating that you can use the Preferences dialog box to enable the welcome screen again. |
| Click **OK** | |
| 3 Choose **File**, **Open...** | |
| Browse to the current unit folder | |
| Open the Outlander Spices folder | |
| Double-click **index.html** | To open the Outlander Spices home page. Home pages are often named index.html, because most Web servers are configured to look for that file name as the Web site's root, or top-level file. |
| 4 Locate the menu bar | The dropdown menus in the menu bar contain commands to perform a wide variety of functions. |
| 5 Locate the Insert bar | The Insert bar provides commands that add elements to a page. The buttons on the Insert bar are shortcuts to the commands in the Insert menu. |
| 6 Locate the Document toolbar | The Document toolbar contains three buttons that control the current view of the open Web page. This toolbar also displays the page title and provides buttons and pop-up menus for frequently used commands. |
| 7 Locate the document window | The document window displays the open Web page. |
| 8 Locate the Property inspector | The Property inspector displays attributes of the selected page element. |
| 9 Locate the Panel groups | The Panel groups enable you to change a variety of Web page properties. |
| 10 Locate the Files panel | The Files panel displays a list of your files and folders. |

| | |
|---|---|
| 11 Click  | (In the document toolbar.) To expand the Visual Aid list. |
| From the list, select **Table Borders** | To hide all table borders used in the layout. |
| 12 Show the table borders again | From the Visual Aid list, select Table Borders. |
| 13 Click 🔍 | (The Zoom tool is in the lower-right corner of the document window.) You'll zoom in on the spices at the top. |

Click as shown

To zoom in on the spices at the top of the page.

| | |
|---|---|
| 14 Click the Zoom list | (In the lower-right corner of the document window.) To display the Zoom list. |
| Select **100%** | |
| 15 Click 🢄 | (The Select tool is in the lower-right corner of the document window.) To return to the default tool. |

## Panel groups

*Explanation*

Each panel group contains individual panels that are represented by tabs, as shown in Exhibit 1-5. You can use these panels to manage file properties or to manage the properties of elements on the current Web page. The following table describes some commonly used panel groups and the panels they contain.

| Panel group | Panels included | Used to... |
|---|---|---|
| Files | Files | Manage site files and folders. |
| | Assets | Manage your site *assets*, such as images, PDFs, or multimedia files. To use the Assets panel, you must first define a local site. |
| | Snippets | Manage *snippets*, which are reusable pieces of HTML code or scripting code. |
| CSS | CSS Styles | Manage the CSS styles of the selected element. This panel is context-sensitive. |
| | AP elements | Manage properties of Absolutely Positioned elements (most commonly <div> tags). |
| Tag inspector | Attributes | Manage every attribute that can be assigned to an HTML tag. |
| | Behaviors | Manage JavaScript code. You can insert JavaScript code to create dynamic and interactive page elements. |

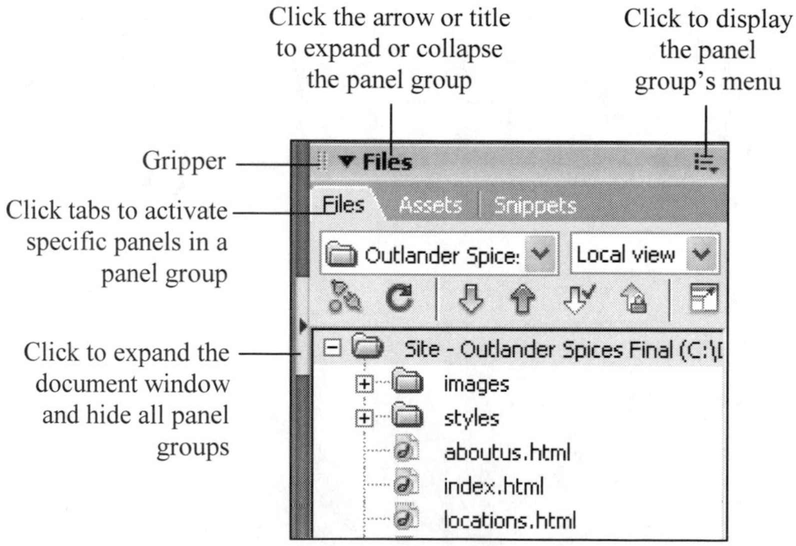

Click the arrow or title to expand or collapse the panel group

Click to display the panel group's menu

Gripper

Click tabs to activate specific panels in a panel group

Click to expand the document window and hide all panel groups

*Exhibit 1-5: The Files panel group*

You can customize the Dreamweaver workspace by manipulating panel groups, as described in the following table.

| To do this... | Do this... |
| --- | --- |
| Hide or display a panel group | Choose Window, and then the name of the panel group. |
| Expand or collapse a panel group | Click its name in the panel group's title bar. |
| Move a panel group to a region of the workspace | Drag from the gripper (in the top-left corner of the panel). |
| Expand a panel group that has been moved in the workspace | Point to the edge of the panel until the pointer changes to a double-sided arrow, and then drag. |
| Hide all panel groups and expand the document window | Click the arrow bar between the document window and the panel groups. |

**Saving a workspace layout**

You can create your own arrangement of panels and then save the custom layout. To save a custom workspace:

1  Arrange the panels in the workspace as desired.
2  Choose Window, Workspace Layout, Save Current to open the Save Workspace Layout dialog box, as shown in Exhibit 1-6.
3  Enter a descriptive name for the workspace and click OK. The new workspace appears in the Workspace Layout submenu.

*Exhibit 1-6: The Save Workspace Layout dialog box*

*Do it!*

## B-2:   Creating a custom workspace

| Here's how | Here's why |
|---|---|
| 1  Locate the Files panel group | This group lists files and folders. It includes panels for Files, Assets, and Snippets. You can use the Files panel to open or move files. |
| Click the title, as shown | ⋮ ▶ Files |
| | To collapse the panel. You'll explore the other panel groups. |
| 2  Expand the CSS panel group | This group includes the CSS Styles and AP Elements panels. |
| Collapse the CSS panel group | Click the title of the CSS panel group. |
| 3  Expand the Application panel group | This group contains the Databases, Bindings, Server Behaviors, and Components panels. |
| Right-click the title of the Application panel | To display a shortcut menu. |
| Choose **Close Panel Group** | To remove the panel group from the display. The Application panel group contains panels that aren't used in this course. |
| 4  Expand the Tag Inspector panel group | (If necessary.) The Tag Inspector panel group includes the Attributes and Behaviors panels. |
| Collapse the Tag Inspector panel group | |
| 5  Expand the Files panel group | You'll use the Files panel to display the site files. |
| In the Files panel, click the Site list and choose **Local Disk (C:)** | (You might need to expand My Computer in the listing.) To select the root directory of the hard drive. You'll navigate to the current unit folder. |
| 6  Point to the gripper, as shown | ⋮▲▼ Files  <br> Files  Assets  Snippets |
| | The pointer changes to a four-sided arrow, indicating that you can move the panel in any direction. |
| Drag the panel group to the center of the workspace | To undock the panel group from the side of the workspace. |

| | | |
|---|---|---|
| 7 | Point to the right edge of the new panel window, as shown | |

The pointer changes to a double-sided arrow, indicating that you can resize the window.

| | | |
|---|---|---|
| | Drag to the right | To enlarge the panel. |
| 8 | Navigate to the current unit folder | |
| | Drag the Files panel group back to the other panel groups | (Drag from the gripper.) You can drag the window anywhere onto the panel groups to re-dock the panel. |
| 9 | Next to the panel groups, click | To hide the panel groups and create more space in which to work in the document window. Clicking the button again shows the panel groups. |
| | Click the arrow button again | To display the panel groups. |
| 10 | Choose **Window**, **Workspace Layout**, **Save Current...** | To open the Save Workspace Layout dialog box. |
| | Type **My Workspace** | |
| | Click **OK** | |
| 11 | Choose **Window**, **Workspace Layout** | To open the Workspace Layout submenu. "My Workspace" appears at the top of the list, making it easy to return to your custom workspace layout, if you make changes to it. |
| | Click away from the menu | |

### The Property inspector

*Explanation*

The Property inspector displays the attributes and properties of the object that's selected in the document window. The expander arrow in the lower-right corner of the Property inspector expands or collapses it to show or hide additional options.

*Do it!*

## B-3: Working with the Property inspector

| Here's how | Here's why |
|---|---|
| 1 In the document window, click **In the News** | You'll use the Property inspector to view the attributes for this text. |
| 2 Observe the Property inspector | The font, style, and other attributes of this text are displayed. |
| 3 In the document window, click the image shown | <br><br>To select it. |
| 4 Observe the Property inspector | The Property inspector displays the attributes of the selected image. |
| 5 Above the Property inspector, click | To hide the Property inspector and expand the document window. |
| At the bottom of the document window, click | To display the Property inspector. The space available in the document window decreases. |

# Topic C:  Editing pages

This topic covers the following Adobe ACE exam objectives for Dreamweaver CS3.

| # | Objective |
|---|-----------|
| 2.6 | List and describe considerations related to designing a site for multiple platforms and browsers. |
| 2.7 | List and describe the features Dreamweaver provides for Accessibility Standards/Section 508 compliance. |
| 2.11 | Given a scenario, set development Preferences. |

### Editing Dreamweaver content

*Explanation*

Editing content in Dreamweaver is a lot like using a word processor. You can add, edit, delete, and rearrange content, such as text and images, on a page. You can save a group of Web pages as a site, similar to saving word processor pages together as a single document. Pages in a word-processor document are typically designed to be read in sequence—when you finish reading page 6, for example, you continue on to page 7. However, pages in a Web site can be linked in any order or in no order at all.

### Web page elements

Web pages can include many types of content, including text, tables, images, and links, as illustrated in Exhibit 1-7.

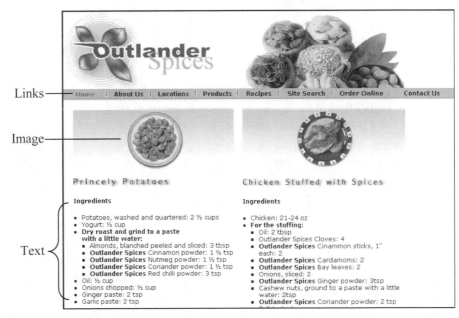

*Exhibit 1-7: A sample Web page*

The following table describes some typical Web page elements.

| Element | Description |
|---|---|
| Text | Words, phrases, sentences, headings, and paragraphs. |
| Table | A grid structure consisting of rows and columns meant primarily to contain tabular data, such as a product list with corresponding prices. Tables can also help you control the layout and spacing of elements on a page. |
| Image | A graphic file, typically in.gif, .jpg, or .png format. Images can also be used as links. |
| Link | Text or an image that directs the browser to another location when clicked. The destination might be another Web page, another area of the current page, or some other resource. |
| Image map | A single graphic that can include multiple links. |
| Forms | Interactive pages consisting of text input fields, check boxes, and buttons that allow the user to submit data to a server for processing and data storage. |

*Do it!*

## C-1: Discussing Web page elements

**Questions and answers**

1 What are links?

2 What's the difference between an image and an image map?

3 What's a table used for?

4 What are forms?

## Text basics

*Explanation*

To add text to a Web page, you can simply type at the insertion point, just as you would in a word-processor. You can also add text by copying and pasting it or dragging it from another application or Web page. After you enter text, you can format it.

Inserting and editing text can sometimes change the position of the text on the page, or it might cause other elements on the page to move. For example, an image that follows a paragraph might move down as more text is added to a paragraph, thus increasing the vertical size of the paragraph.

*Do it!*

## C-2: Inserting and editing text

| Here's how | Here's why |
|---|---|
| 1 In the top paragraph, click to the left of **spices**, as shown | heritage of &#124;spices from all<br>d specialty stores all over |
| | To place the insertion point at this location. |
| 2 Type **the finest** | To add text to the paragraph. |
| Press (SPACEBAR) | To add a space. This type of text editing is no different from working in a word processor. |
| 3 Place the insertion point as shown | **Featured Products**&#124; |
| | Only one product is currently featured, so you'll delete the "s" in "Products." |
| Press (← BACKSPACE) | To delete the letter. |
| 4 Choose **File**, **Save** | To update the document. |

## Basic text formatting

*Explanation*  Unless you set a font face and other text styles, any text that you add to a page uses the browser's default font. Using the Property inspector, you can quickly format text to suit your design and improve readability.

### Basic text attributes

Although you can format text using menu commands in the Text menu, it's generally easier to use the Property inspector. When you place the insertion point in a paragraph or select a specific portion of text, the Property inspector displays the selection's current styles and additional formatting options, as shown in Exhibit 1-8. Select options from the Format, Font, Style, and Size lists to format text as desired. For example, you can select a font set from the Font list to change the existing one, and you can click the Bold or Italic buttons to apply additional styles.

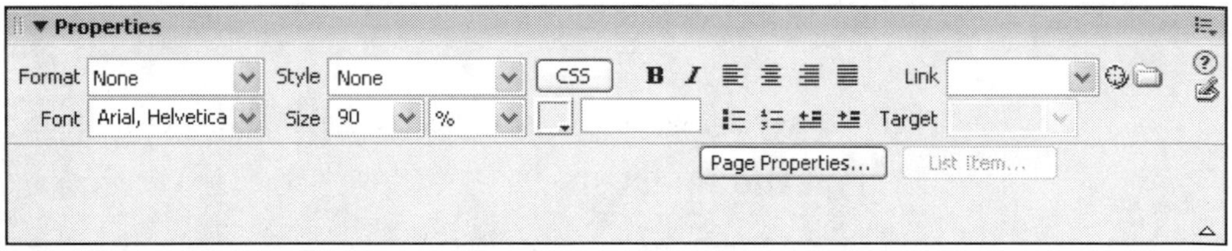

*Exhibit 1-8: Text attributes in the Property inspector*

### Font sets

A *font set* is a group of similar fonts, an example of which is shown in Exhibit 1-9. When you apply a font set, the user's Web browser attempts to display the text in the first font specified in the set. If the first font isn't available on the user's computer, it uses the second font in the set. If that font isn't available, it attempts to apply the third font, and so on. A font set should end with a generic font specification, serif, sans-serif, or monospaced. This guarantees that, even if a user doesn't have any of the fonts listed in your font set, at least the general font type displays.

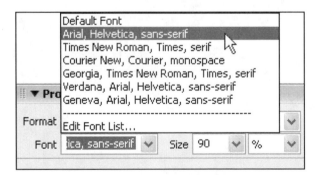

*Exhibit 1-9: Font sets available in the Font list in the Property inspector*

The difference between serif and sans-serif fonts is the style in which the letters are formed. A serif font has *flourishes* (decorations) at the ends of its characters, while sans-serif fonts don't. These differences are illustrated by the examples in Exhibit 1-10. Monospace fonts are font faces such as Courier and Courier New, which have the same amount of space between all characters and resemble typewriter text.

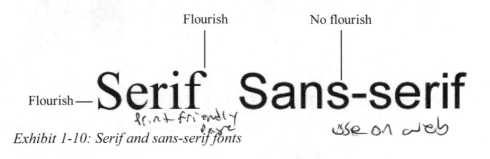

*Exhibit 1-10: Serif and sans-serif fonts*

### Selecting text

There are several ways you can select text for editing or formatting:

- Drag across the text you want to select.
- Click a word twice to select the whole word.
- Click three times anywhere in a paragraph to select that paragraph.

*Do it!*

## C-3: Formatting text

| Here's how | Here's why |
|---|---|
| 1 Triple-click the first paragraph | |

We bring you a r
find o[ ] kiosks in
order directly fro[ ]
exceptional quali[ ]

Discover a whole
store near you!

To select it. You'll apply a font set to this text.

Choose **Text**, **Font**, **Georgia**, **Times New Roman**, **Times**, **serif**

To apply the Georgia font set to the selected text. The last font in this set is serif. This generic font declaration ensures that, at the very least, the type of font you want is applied, no matter what fonts are available on the user's system.

2 In the Property inspector, click the Font list and choose **Verdana**, **Arial**, **Helvetica**, **sans-serif**

Georgia, Times New R[
Verdana, Arial, Helvet[
Geneva, Arial Helveti[
----------------------------
Edit Font List...
Font  ca, sans-serif

To apply the Verdana font set to the selected text. The other text on the page uses this font set also.

3 Select the first sentence under the Awards heading

Awards

Outlander Spices has won the prestigious IS
certification for producing quality spices. Thi[
reflects the company commitment to provide

In the Property inspector, click **B**

(The Bold button.) To make the selected text bold.

4 Save the page

Choose File, Save or press Ctrl+S.

## Adding images

*Explanation*
Web designers often use images to convey or reinforce ideas in ways that text alone can't. A Web page that includes images is typically more visually appealing and inviting to the user than is a page with just text.

To insert an image in a Web page:

1  If necessary, create a subfolder in the site folder and place all the image files within it.

2  In the Files panel, navigate to the folder containing the images for the current site.

3  Drag an image file to the document window.

4  In the Image Tag Accessibility Attributes dialog box, type alternate text, and click OK.

You can then adjust the size and position of an image using the options in the Property inspector.

### Alternate text

When you add an image, Dreamweaver prompts you to provide alternate text for the image. Users that have images disabled in their browsers or who use non-visual browsers will be able to read the alternate text and understand its context in the document. If you point to an image that has alternate text, some browsers show the text as a tooltip. Alternate text should describe either the content or the purpose of the image—whichever is most appropriate.

*Do it!*
### C-4:    Adding an image

| Here's how | Here's why |
| --- | --- |
| 1  Scroll to the bottom of the page | You'll insert an image to the left of the Awards heading. |
| 2  In the Files panel, navigate to the images folder | In the Outlander folder, in the current unit folder. |
| Drag **iso.jpg** to the document window, as shown | Awards<br>Outlander Spi<br>9000 certificat<br>This award refl |
| | To place the image on the page. The Image Tag Accessibility Attributes dialog box appears. |
| In the Alternate text box, type **ISO 9000 Award** | To assign an alternate text string to this image. |
| Click **OK** | To close the Image Tag Accessibility Attributes dialog box. |
| 3  Save the page | |

## Previewing a Web page

*Explanation*

To preview a Web page in a browser:

1 In the Document toolbar, click the "Preview/Debug in browser" button.
2 From the dropdown list that appears, select a browser. The Adobe Dreamweaver CS3 dialog box appears.
3 Click No to preview the page in its saved state. Click Yes to save the page first and then preview it.

### Adding browsers

Not all browsers display a Web page the same way—there are often minor differences in how each browser interprets HTML and CSS code, and these differences can affect the way a page looks and functions. For this reason, it's a good idea to preview your Web pages in several browsers. When you first install Dreamweaver, it detects the browsers installed on your computer. It uses your default browser as the primary browser for previewing pages. You can also add other browsers as needed.

To add other browsers to the Preview list:

1 Choose Edit, Preferences (or press Ctrl + U) to open Preferences dialog box.
2 In the Category list, select Preview in Browser.
3 Click the plus sign next to Browsers to open the Add Browser dialog box.
4 In the Name box, type a name for the browser.
5 Click the Browse button, and navigate to the .exe file for the desired browser (typically located in a folder in the C:\Program Files folder).
6 Check Secondary browser.
7 Click OK to close the Add Browser dialog box.
8 Repeat steps 3–7 for each browser you want to add to the preview menu.
9 Click OK to close the Preferences dialog box.

*Do it!*

## C-5: Previewing a page in a browser

| Here's how | Here's why |
|---|---|
| 1 In the document toolbar, click [icon] | (The "Preview/Debug in browser" button.) A drop-down list appears. |
| Select **Preview in IExplore** | To view the page in Internet Explorer. The Adobe Dreamweaver CS3 dialog box appears. |
| Click **Yes** | To save the page in its current state. The page appears in Internet Explorer. |
| 2 Close the browser | |

# Topic D:  Code tools

This topic covers the following Adobe ACE exam objectives for Dreamweaver CS3.

| # | Objective |
|---|-----------|
| 1.1 | Given an HTML tag, explain the purpose of that tag. (Tags include: <div> <span> <table> <a>.) |
| 3.17 | Given a coding tool or feature, describe the purpose of or how to use that tool or feature. (Tools or features include: Code and Design View, Code Collapse, Code Navigation, Code Hinting, Coding Context Menu option.) |

## HTML code

*Explanation*

As you learned earlier, HTML code encloses your text content and defines the basic structure of a Web page. Even if you prefer to work in Design view, you need to be familiar with basic HTML syntax.

### Standard tags

Tags define a document's basic structure. A *tag* is a command that tells the browser how to interpret or display the content enclosed by the tag. For example, the <h1> tag identifies a line of text as a level-one heading, and the browser renders it accordingly.

HTML tags are enclosed in angle brackets: < >. Most HTML tags consist of a beginning tag and an ending tag. The ending tag includes a forward slash (/), which tells the browser that the tag instruction has ended. For example, the following code is a snippet of text that uses the <b> tag to define bold text:

```
Outlander Spices makes the <b>best</b> seasonings.
```

A Web browser would display this text as follows:

Outlander Spices makes the **best** seasonings.

The following code shows the basic structure of an HTML document. Notice that some tags are nested inside other tags, and there's an ending tag for each starting tag.

```
<html>
  <head>
    <title>Document Title</title>
  </head>
  <body>
    All rendered HTML and content is inserted here.
  </body>
</html>
```

The standard tags that begin every HTML document are <html>, <head>, and <body>. The <html> element is considered the *root element,* or top-level element. All other HTML tags reside within the <html> tag. It defines the document as an HTML document. Every HTML document is then divided into two sections: the <head> section and the <body> section.

The <head> section contains the <title> element, which defines the document's title. This section also contains style sheet information, meta information, scripts, and other code or resources that aren't rendered on the page.

The <body> section contains all the content (text, images, etc.) that's rendered on a page, along with the code for it. If you can see it in a browser, the code for it is in the body section.

Each tag in the <body> section performs a specific function to define the content. The following table describes a few of the most commonly used HTML tags.

| Tag | Description |
| --- | --- |
| <a> | Creates a hyperlink to another page or site. |
| <div> | Defines a section (division) of a page and allows all elements within that section to share formatting attributes. |
| <span> | Allows you to attach style attributes to an inline section of text. For example, specific words or phrases within a paragraph. |
| <table> | Creates a table. |

## Document views

You can view the HTML code for a page using the view buttons at the top of the document window, as shown in Exhibit 1-11. Design view is selected by default. You can view the code by clicking the Code button, or you can click the Split button to split the window into Design view and Code view.

*Exhibit 1-11: View buttons at the top of a document window*

### The Coding toolbar

When you view a page in Code view, the Coding toolbar is visible on the left side of the document window, as shown in Exhibit 1-12. You can use the Coding toolbar to perform common coding tasks, such as indenting code, expanding and collapsing code sections, and adding and removing comments.

### The Shortcut menu

Code view provides a shortcut menu of frequently used commands. To use the shortcut menu, right-click anywhere within the code to display the menu, and then choose a command or function.

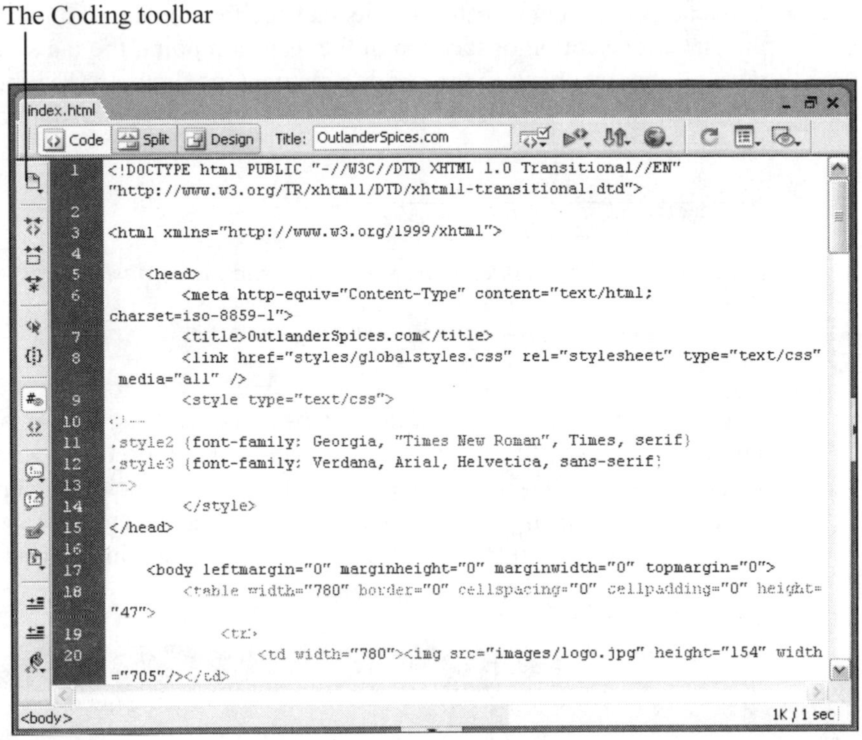

The Coding toolbar

*Exhibit 1-12: The Coding toolbar*

### The Reference panel

As you work in Code view, there are likely to be times when you need information about certain tags or attributes to understand and fix errors better. To access information about specific tags, right-click the tag in Code view and choose Reference. This opens the Reference panel, as shown in Exhibit 1-13, with information about the selected tag. You can also search for information using the Book and Tag lists at the top of the panel.

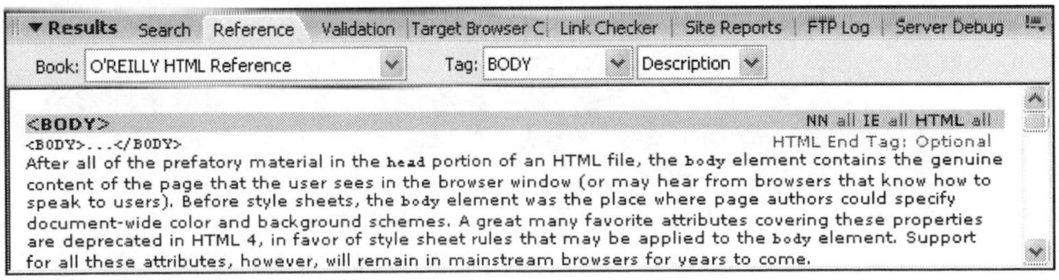

*Exhibit 1-13: The Reference panel*

### The tag selector

You can use the tag selector to select a specific element and its contents. Depending on the current selection or location of the insertion point, the tag selector shows the parent tags, all the way back to the <body> element, as shown in Exhibit 1-14. The tag selector is in the lower-left corner of the Document window and is visible in both Code view and Design view.

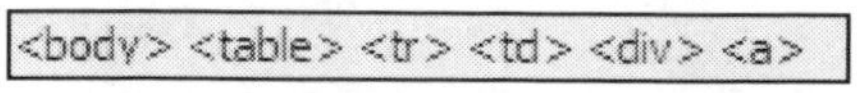

<body> <table> <tr> <td> <div> <a>

*Exhibit 1-14: The tag selector, showing a sample of nested tags*

### The Tag Editor

You can manipulate code in Design view, using the Tag Editor, shown in Exhibit 1-15. To open the Tag Editor, right-click selected content on the page, and then choose Edit Tag <tag> (the <tag> in the menu corresponds to the selected content.) You can also choose Modify, Edit Tag. To make changes, select a category on the left and make the necessary changes on the right side. You can also obtain information about tags using the Tag Info toggle in the lower-right corner. 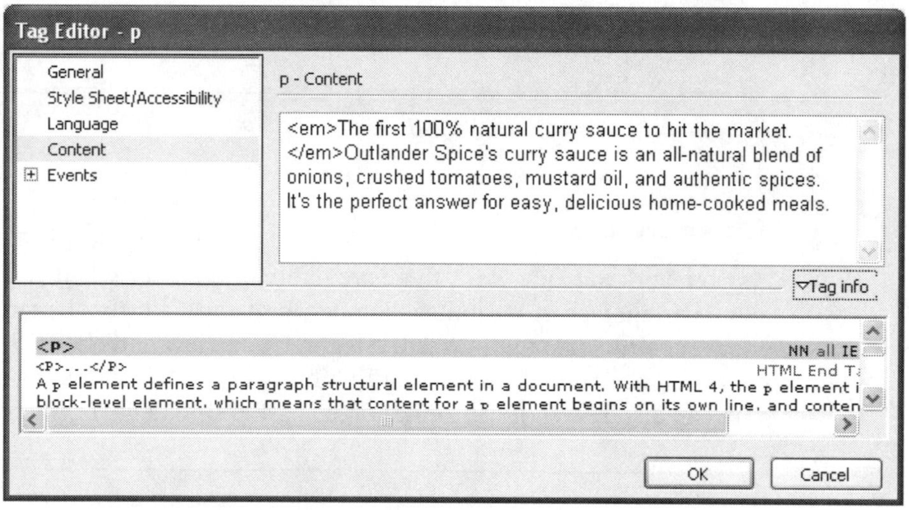

**Tag Editor - p**

General
Style Sheet/Accessibility
Language
Content
⊞ Events

p - Content

<em>The first 100% natural curry sauce to hit the market. </em>Outlander Spice's curry sauce is an all-natural blend of onions, crushed tomatoes, mustard oil, and authentic spices. It's the perfect answer for easy, delicious home-cooked meals.

▽Tag info

**<P>**                                                                 NN all IE
<P>...</P>                                                       HTML End Ta
A p element defines a paragraph structural element in a document. With HTML 4, the p element i
block-level element. which means that content for a p element begins on its own line. and conten

OK      Cancel

*Exhibit 1-15: The Tag Editor*

*Do it!*     **D-1:   Exploring code tools**

| Here's how | Here's why |
|---|---|
| 1  Click  [⊞ Split] | (On the Document toolbar.) To split the document window into Code view and Design view. |
| 2  In Design view, click an image on the page | To select it. Code view automatically highlights the code that defines the selected object. |
| 3  Click  [‹› Code] | To switch to Code view. |
| 4  Locate the `<head>` tag  What's the purpose of this element? | |
| 5  Locate the `<body>` tag  What's the purpose of this element? | |
| 6  Under the `<body>` tag, right click the first `<table>` tag | ```
<body>
<img src="images/logo
<table width="100%" b
  <t    Edit Tag <table>...
        Insert Tag...
href    Functions
```  A shortcut menu appears. |
|   From the menu, choose **Reference** | The Reference panel appears at the bottom of the window, and a description of the `<table>` tag appears. |
| 7  Right-click the Results panel group tab, and choose **Close panel group** | ```
▼ R
       Help
Bod
       Group Reference with    ▶
       Close Reference
<TA
<TAl   Rename panel group...
The
con    Maximize panel group
the    Close panel group
with
of the structure of tr and td elem
```  To close the panel group. |
| 8  Triple-click the `<table>` tag | To select the entire line of code. |

9  In the Coding toolbar, click ⟨⟩   (The Collapse Full Tag button.) To collapse everything between the opening and closing ⟨table⟩ tags.

Click as shown

```
14    <body>
15    <img src="ima
16 ⌐  <table ...
21    <table width=
22      <tr>
```

To expand the tags again.

10  Click ⟨Design⟩   To switch to Design view. You'll also edit some code in Design view using shortcut menus.

11  Under "In the News," click anywhere in the first paragraph   To place the insertion point.

In the tag selector, click ⟨p⟩, as shown

```
<body> <table> <tr> <td> <table> <tr> <td> <p>
▼ Properties
```

Right-click the selected paragraph and choose **Edit Tag ⟨p⟩...**   The Tag Editor appears. By default, the General category is selected. The only option for the ⟨p⟩ tag in the General category is alignment.

12  In the lower-right corner, click Tag info, as shown

```
▷ Tag info
Cancel
```

To expand the dialog box and view reference information for the ⟨p⟩ tag.

Briefly scan the information on the paragraph tag

13  In the category list, select **Content**   The content of the selected paragraph appears. You can add HTML tags in the Content window.

14  Make the first sentence in the paragraph bold, as shown

```
p - Content
<b>The first 100% natural curry sauce to hit the market.</b>
Outlander Spice's curry sauce is an all-natural blend of onion
```

Insert an opening ⟨b⟩ tag at the start of the paragraph and a closing ⟨/b⟩ tag at the end of the first sentence.

Click **OK**   To close the dialog box.

Deselect the paragraph   (Click anywhere on the page.) To view the changes. The first sentence in the paragraph is now bold.

15  Save and close the page

# Unit summary: Getting started

**Topic A**    In this topic, you learned a few basics about the **Internet**, the **World Wide Web**, and **HTML**. You learned that HTML and XHTML are standard **markup languages** used to build Web pages, and that Dreamweaver uses XHTML code by default.

**Topic B**    In this topic, you identified the main components of the **Dreamweaver CS3 workspace**, including panel groups and the Property inspector.

**Topic C**    In this topic, you learned how to perform basic editing, including inserting and formatting text and adding images. You also learned how to apply basic **font styles** and preview a page in a browser.

**Topic D**    In this topic, you learned how to use Dreamweaver's **code tools**, and you learned more about **HTML tags**, including basic HTML syntax and the fundamental tags that define the structure of a Web page.

## Independent practice activity

In this activity, you'll insert and format text and preview the page in Internet Explorer. Then you'll make a basic formatting change and view the results.

1  From the current unit folder, open the Practice folder.

2  Open index.html and save it as **Myindex.html**.

3  Fix the link for the logo.jpg image. (*Hint:* The image is in the "images" subfolder.)

4  View the source code. (Use either Code view or Split view.)

5  Switch back to Design view.

6  Add some text of your choice to the document.

7  Format the new text with a font set of your choice.

8  Save the page and preview it in Internet Explorer. When you're done, return to Dreamweaver without closing the browser window.

9  Make the text you added bold.

10  Save the page and refresh the browser to view the results.

11  Close the browser to return to Dreamweaver.

12  Close Myindex.html

## Review questions

1 Which are ways you can zoom in on a document page? [Choose all that apply.]

   A Select the Zoom tool and click the page.

   B Use the Select tool to drag a marquee over the area you want to magnify.

   C Right-click anywhere on the page, then choose a preset magnification setting.

   D Display the Zoom list and select a magnification value.

2 How can you hide table borders?

   A Right-click inside the table, then choose Table, Hide Table Borders.

   B Double-click the table border.

   C Select the table, then choose View, Hide Table Borders.

   D Deselect the Table Borders option in the Visual Aids list in the document toolbar.

3 How can you add an image to a page?

   A Drag the image file from the Files panel to the document window.

   B In the Files panel, right-click the image and choose Insert.

   C Choose File, Import, then navigate to the location of the image file and click OK.

   D In the Files panel, double-click the image file.

4 What are the three fundamental HTML tags that must be used on every Web page?

   A `<title>`, `<head>`, `<body>`

   B `<html>`, `<head>`, `<body>`

   C `<start>`, `<body>`, `<end>`

   D `<html>`, `<head>`, `<content>`

5 Which shows the correct syntax to make text bold?

   A <b>Outlander Spices<b>

   B <b>Outlander Spices

   C <b>Outlander Spices<b/>

   D <b>Outlander Spices</b>

6 How can you view the code for a document? [Choose all that apply.]

   A Press Ctrl+`

   B Click the Code button at the top of the document window.

   C Press F5.

   D Click the Split button at the top of the document window.

7 You're currently viewing a page in Design view. How can you view the Coding toolbar?

   A  Switch to Code view.

   B  Choose View, Toolbars, Coding.

   C  Choose Window, Code Inspector.

   D  Choose View, Code View Options, Coding.

8 In Code view, how can you collapse a selected tag? [Choose all that apply.]

   A  Choose Modify, Collapse Full Tag.

   B  In the Coding toolbar, click the Collapse Full Tag button.

   C  Double-click the tag.

   D  To the left of the tag, click the small minus (-) sign.

9 Which panel provides specific information about HTML tags?

   A  Validation panel.

   B  Search panel.

   C  Snippets panel.

   D  Reference panel.

10 How can you open the Tag Editor for selected content? [Choose all that apply.]

   A  Double-click the selected content.

   B  Right-click the selected content, and then choose Edit Tag <tag>.

   C  Choose Modify, Edit Tag.

   D  Choose Edit, Select Parent Tag.

# Unit 2

## Web sites and pages

**Unit time: 30 minutes**

Complete this unit, and you'll know how to:

**A** Plan and define a Web site, and work with the Files panel and Assets panel.

**B** Create a Web page, import text from external files, and set page properties.

# Topic A:  Creating a Web site

This topic covers the following Adobe ACE exam objectives for Dreamweaver CS3.

| # | Objective |
|---|-----------|
| 2.2 | Manage site definitions for local, remote, and testing server information. |
| 2.4 | Given a scenario, define the structure of a site. |
| 2.6 | List and describe considerations related to designing a site for multiple platforms and browsers. |
| 2.11 | Given a scenario, set development Preferences. |

### Site planning and organization

*Explanation*

Organizing site files in a logical structure is critical to the successful operation of your Web site. The structure of a Web site also affects a developer's ability to maintain the site efficiently over time.

### Planning

When you start creating a Web site, you might be inclined first to write content for the pages. But it's best to plan your Web site carefully first. Think about how best to structure your pages and content, how you want to present information, and how you want the site to look (color schemes, fonts, and so on) before you begin working on individual pages. Spend some time defining the audience for the site and the goals you want to accomplish with it.

Effective design also results in easier maintenance. Content requirements, design changes, and job assignments typically change over time. You should plan and design a site that will be easy for another developer or team of developers to take over.

#### Site structure

A well-designed site must have an effective navigation scheme. You need to plan the link relationships between the pages in your site. Sometimes you can prevent problems by drafting a site flowchart, similar to the simple example in Exhibit 2-1.

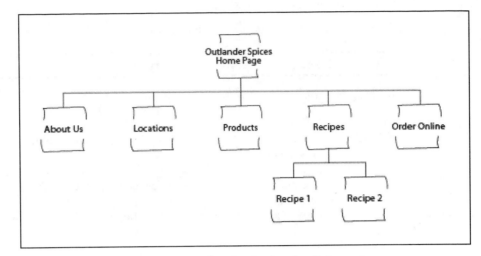

*Exhibit 2-1: A sample flowchart for the Outlander Spices site*

You should also keep all the files you plan to use in the site in a logical, organized folder structure. Exhibit 2-2 shows a typical folder structure for a Web site. All images are stored in their own folder, and styles, scripts, and multimedia files are also stored separately in logically named folders.

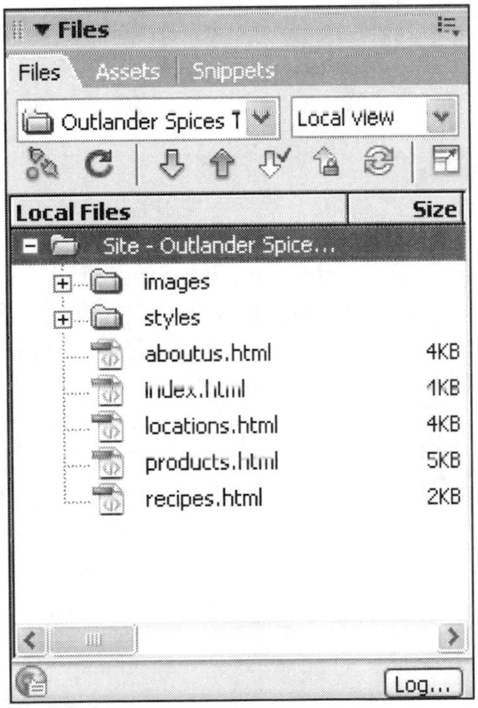

*Exhibit 2-2: Typical folder structure for a Web site*

### Sites: local, remote, and testing

When planning a site, you should define three folders for your site files:

| Folder | Location | Purpose |
| --- | --- | --- |
| Local | Your local hard disk | To store work in progress. You transfer files from the local sites to the other sites when they're complete. |
| Remote | The Web server where your site is published | To make your site available to your intended audience. |
| Testing | Any computer; including your local PC, the Web server, or a testing server. | To test your connection to databases and to test dynamic pages (pages that change according to information received from databases or page variables). |

The local folder on your computer is where you work on the site before you publish it on the Web. After you verify that it looks and functions as you intend, you can publish it to a remote folder on the Web server that hosts your site.

If your site includes *dynamic content* (pages or information that can change in response to information received from databases, user activity, or other variables), then you should also define a testing folder.

A *local site* serves as the root directory for your Web site. When defining the site's root folder, don't use the root of your hard drive or the Dreamweaver application folder.

To define a local site:

1 Choose Site, New Site to open the Site Definition dialog box, shown in Exhibit 2-3.

2 In the Site name box, enter a name for the site.

3 In the Local root folder box, enter the URL for the site. You can click the folder icon to the right of the box to navigate to the folder.

4 Click Next, and complete the screens for the Site Definition Wizard. The last screen displays a summary.

5 Click Done to create the site.

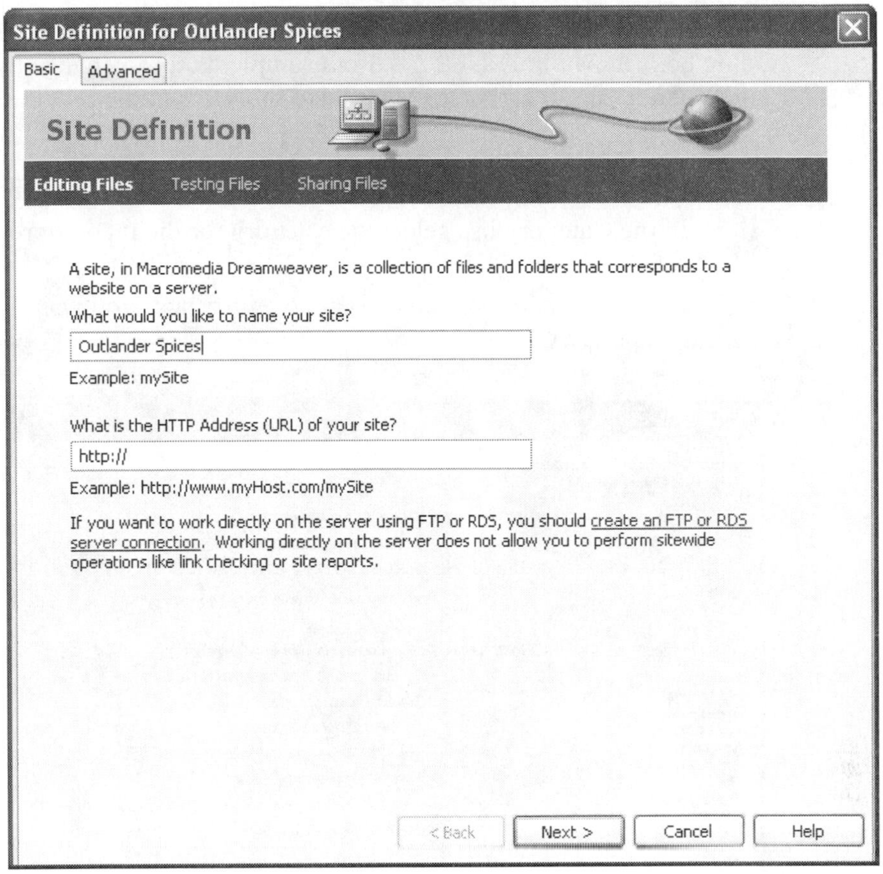

*Exhibit 2-3: The Site Definition dialog box*

**Planning for multiple platforms and browsers**

If the audience for your site uses a common platform, such as an internal corporate network, then you can design your site for the specifics of that platform. But users on the Web have a wide variety of operating systems and browsers. Keep the following considerations in mind to help ensure that your site displays and functions properly in all browsers:

- Different browsers might interpret CSS and even some HTML differently. You should download and install a variety of browsers so that you can test your site and your pages for a diverse Web audience. Recent statistics suggest that over 90% of Web users use some version of Microsoft Internet Explorer or Mozilla Firefox. Other browsers include Safari, Netscape, and Opera.

- Dreamweaver provides behaviors (rollovers and other actions) that are written in javascript, for use in modern browsers. These behaviors include "workaround" coding, so that they fail gracefully in older browsers that don't support javascript, or when users disable javascript in their browsers. Use these behaviors as they're written; editing them may disable the workarounds.

- The Macintosh, UNIX, and Windows operating systems each use different end-of-line characters. If the remote server that hosts your site uses an operating system that's different from the one on your computer, you should specify a Line Break Type for the remote server by using the Preferences dialog box's Code Format category.

**Setting preferences**

You can change a variety of default settings in Dreamweaver by using the Preferences dialog box, shown in Exhibit 2-4. For example, you can change the way Dreamweaver copies and pastes content, or you can add browsers to the preview list.

To set preferences:

1 Choose Edit, Preferences to open the Preferences dialog box.

2 In the Category list, select the category for the type of preferences you want to set.

3 Use the category options to set the preferences you want.

4 Click OK.

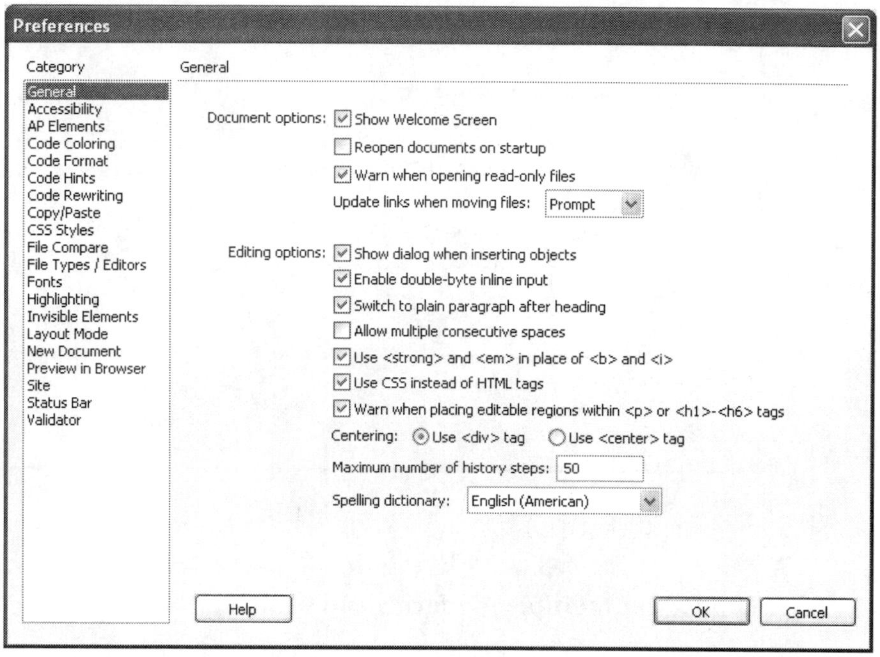

*Exhibit 2-4: The Preferences dialog box*

Several commonly used preference categories include:

| Category | Options Provided |
|---|---|
| General | To adjust general Dreamweaver attributes, such as showing/hiding the startup page, or activating certain pages on startup. You can also control editing options, such as allowing multiple spaces in text or using CSS instead of HTML attributes for some style options. |
| Code Format | To change the appearance of your code by specifying formatting options, such as indentation, line length, and the line break type. |
| Copy/Paste | To control the way Dreamweaver copies and pastes content from other applications. |
| CSS Styles | To control the way Dreamweaver writes CSS code. |
| New Document | To change the default document type Dreamweaver generates when you create a new document (that is, HTML, XHTML, ASP, JSP), also to change the file extension applied (that is, HTML vs. HTM.) |
| Preview in Browser | To control the way Dreamweaver previews pages in a browser or in multiple browsers. |

**The Assets panel**

Dreamweaver keeps track of your site's *assets*, which are the components of your site, such as images or multimedia files. The Assets panel, shown in Exhibit 2-5, displays a list of images and other assets and displays information about each file, such as its dimensions, file size, file type, and path.

*Exhibit 2-5: The Assets panel*

*Do it!*                    **A-1:   Defining a site**

| Here's how | Here's why |
|---|---|
| 1  Choose **Site**, **New Site...** | To open the Site Definition Wizard. You'll create a Web site. |
| 2  For the site name, enter **Outlander Spices** | To name the Web site. As you type, this name appears in the Wizard's title bar. |
| Set the HTTP address to **http://www.outlanderspices.com** | |
| Click **Next** | |
| 3  Verify that **No**, **I do not want to use a server technology** is selected | |
| Click **Next** | The Editing Files, Part 3 screen appears. |
| 4  Verify that **Edit local copies on my machine** is selected | |
| Click 🗀 | To open the "Choose local root folder for site Outlander Spices" dialog box. |
| 5  Browse to the Outlander Spices folder | In the current unit folder. |
| Open the folder and click **Select** | To specify where the files for this site should be stored. |
| 6  Activate the Advanced tab | You'll observe the settings for remote and testing servers. |
| In the Category list, select **Remote Info** | |
| Display the Access list | To observe the options for connecting to a remote server. |
| Select **None** | You don't need to connect to a remote server for this activity. |

7  In the Category list, select
**Testing Server**

   Observe the selections in the two lists

In addition to an Access list that determines how you connect to a testing server, there's a Server model list that determines the type of server technology that's used by the testing server.

   Verify that both lists are set to **None**

| Server model: | None | ∨ |
|---|---|---|
| Access: | None | ∨ |

   Activate the Basic tab

To continue setting up the local site.

   Click **Next**

The Summary screen appears.

8  Click **Done**

To create the site.

9  Observe the Files panel

Outlander Spices is listed as a Web site.

   Verify that the Site folder is expanded, showing the site folders and files

| Files | Assets | Snippets |
|---|---|---|

| 📁 Outlander Spices ∨ | Local view ∨ |
|---|---|

| **Local Files** | **Size** |
|---|---|
| ⊟ 📁  Site - Outlander Spices (... | |
| ⊞ 📁   images | |
| ⊞ 📁   styles | |
| 📄   aboutus.html | 9KB |
| 📄   booksinfo1.doc | 19KB |
| 📄   booksinfo2.txt | 1KB |
| 📄   index.html | 4KB |
| 📄   locations.html | 4KB |

10  Detach the Files panel group

(Drag from the panel group's gripper to the center of the screen.) The Files panel group appears in a separate window.

11  Activate the Assets panel

(At the top of the Files panel group, click Assets.) By default, the images in the site display in the Assets panel.

   Click ▦

To view the colors in use in the site.

   Click 🖼

To view the site's images again.

12  Enlarge the Files panel group

Point to the bottom-right corner of the panel group until the pointer changes to a double-sided arrow, and then drag to the right.

| 13 | Observe the Files panel group | To view the file information for each asset. |

| 14 | Drag the Files panel group back under the docked panel groups | |
| | Activate the Files panel | To return to the list of site files. |
| 15 | Choose **Edit**, **Preferences...** | To open the Preferences dialog box. You'll view the line break type for the remote server. |
| | In the Category list, select **Code Format** | |
| | Observe the selections in the Line break type list | |

```
CR LF (Windows)
CR (Macintosh)
LF (Unix)
```

| 16 | Verify that CR LF (Windows) is selected | To format your site with line breaks for a remote server that uses Windows. |
| | Click **OK** | To close the dialog box. |

# Topic B:   Creating Web pages

This topic covers the following Adobe ACE exam objectives for Dreamweaver CS3.

| # | Objective |
|---|---|
| **2.5** | Given a scenario, select and set the appropriate resolution for a site. |
| **2.9** | Create pages by using CSS starter pages. |
| **2.11** | Given a scenario, set development Preferences. |
| **3.9** | List and describe the options for creating and saving new pages. |
| **3.10** | Set document properties by using the Document Properties dialog box. |

## Web pages

*Explanation*

Dreamweaver makes it easy to add pages to a Web site. There are several ways you can create new Web pages, as described in the following table.

| Option | Description |
|---|---|
| Blank page | You can create a new blank HTML page that contains only the basic document structure with no content. You can also create a blank page that contains dummy content in a preset layout that you can modify to suit your own site. In the Blank Page category of the New Document dialog box, you can also create CSS documents, XML documents, and many other document types. |
| Blank Template | This set of options provides HTML templates, as well as templates for server technologies, such as ASP.NET and ColdFusion. |
| Page from Template | This option shows a list of your own templates from which you can create new pages |
| Page from Sample | This option provides dozens of pre-built style sheets and starter pages built with layout themes that you can use and modify. |

### Create a basic page

To create a basic HTML page:

1   Choose File, New to open the New Document dialog box.
2   Select Blank Page.
3   From the Page Type list, select HTML.
4   Click Create.

**Page titles**

You should give every page a title, which appears in the title bar of the browser window. Exhibit 2-6 shows the title of a page viewed in various browsers. To specify a page title, enter the title in the Title box on the Document toolbar.

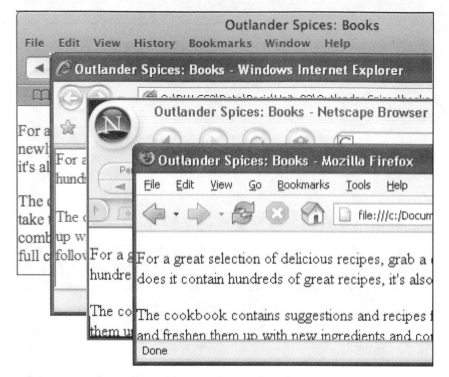

*Exhibit 2-6: Page titles as they appear in four browsers*

**The Window Size pop-up menu**

At the bottom of the document window, there's a Window Size pop-up menu that you can use to view pages at various dimensions. The dimensions on the left side of the menu represent the actual space within the browser window, and the dimensions on the right represent the monitor resolution.

To activate the Window Size pop-up menu, click anywhere on the current resolution numbers shown at the bottom of the document window. When the document window is maximized, the pop-up menu is disabled. To change the dimensions of the document window, you need to float the document window, click the dimension numbers, and then select another option from the menu.

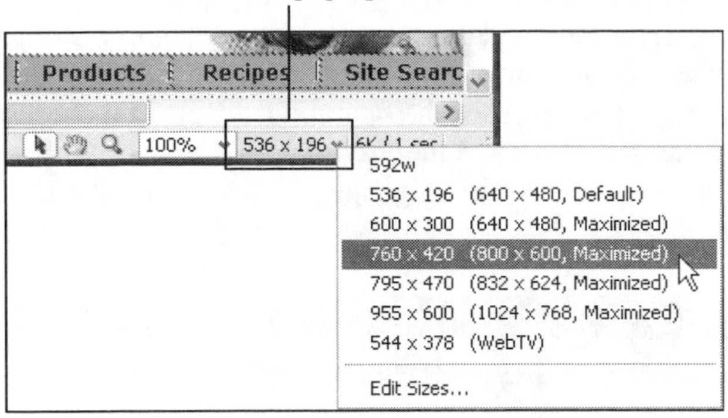

Window Size pop-up menu

*Exhibit 2-7: The Window Size pop-up menu*

The Window Size pop-up menu can be helpful when you want to view your layout as it appears at a specific resolution. Most developers design pages for 1024x768, which is the default resolution of many monitors.

### Starter pages

You can quickly create professional-looking pages by using starter pages. *Starter pages* are pre-built CSS layouts with fictional content, which you can modify with your own content. To access these pages, select Page from Sample in the New Document dialog box, and then select Starter Page (Theme), as shown in Exhibit 2-8. You can preview each theme by selecting it in the Sample Page list.

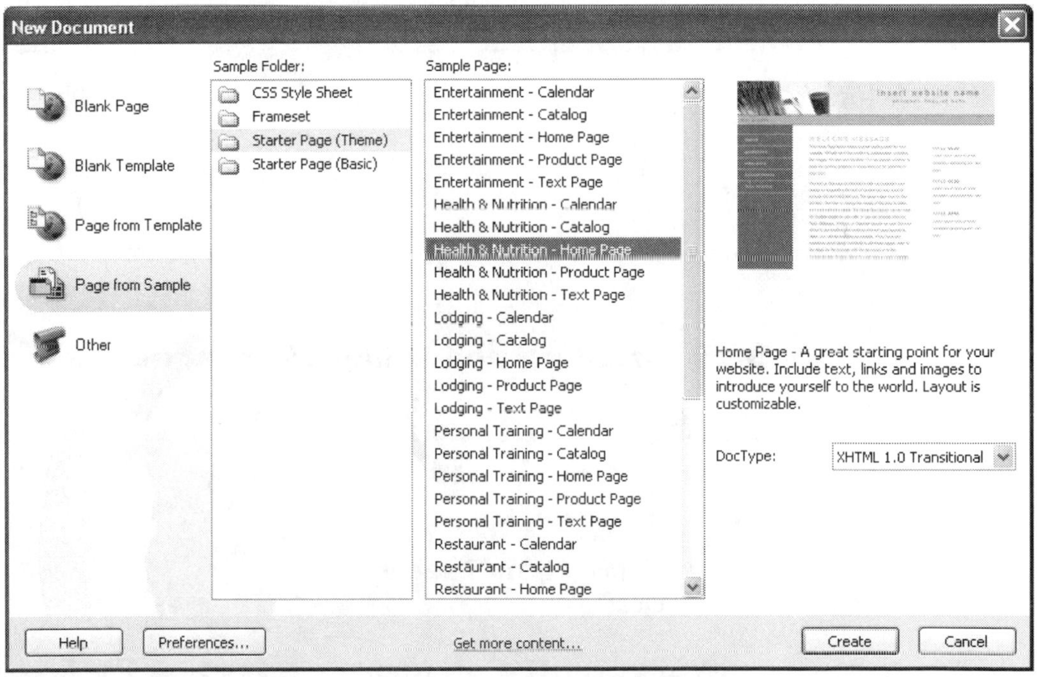

*Exhibit 2-8: Starter pages in the New Document dialog box*

**Language support**

Dreamweaver supports many languages. However, to design pages for other languages, you need to specify a language for the operating system you're using and select the appropriate encoding option for the language in Dreamweaver. You can use the Control Panel to change the language for the operating system. To change the language encoding in Dreamweaver, open the Preferences dialog box, then select the New Document category. Choose the language you want from the Default encoding list, as shown in Exhibit 2-9.

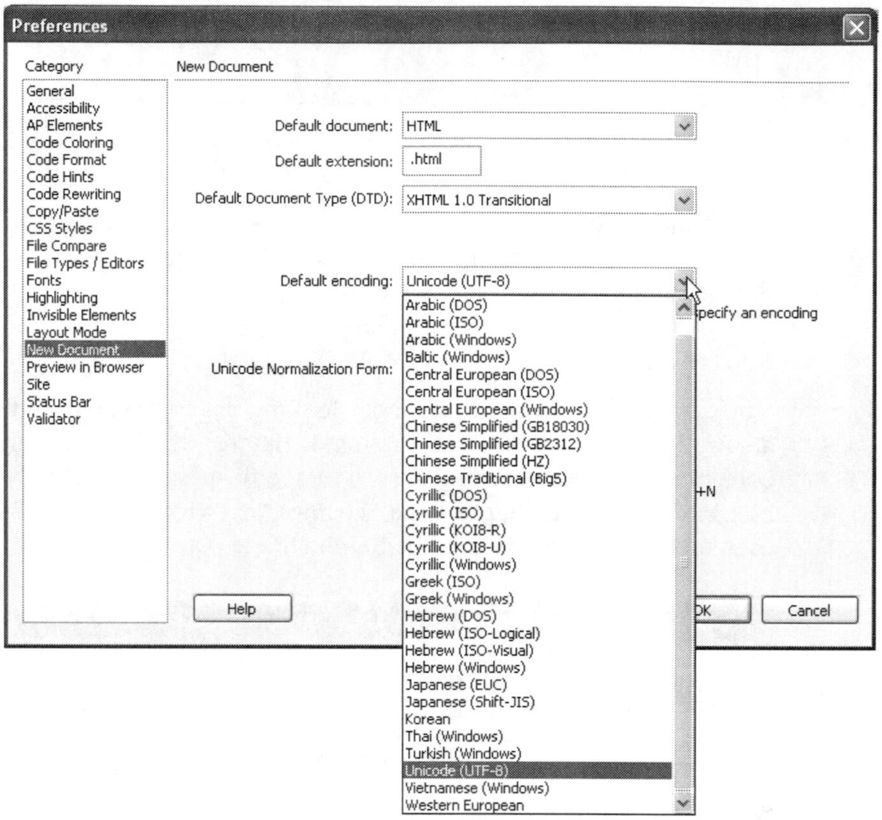

*Exhibit 2-9: Setting encoding preferences for languages*

*Do it!*

## B-1: Creating and titling Web pages

| Here's how | Here's why |
|---|---|
| 1 Choose **File, New...** | To start creating a Web page. The New Document dialog box appears. |
| Verify that **Blank Page** is selected | |
| Verify that **HTML** and **<none>** are selected | In the Page Type list and Layout list, respectively. |
| Click **Create** | To open a blank HTML page. |

2  Open the Window Size pop-up menu

(Click the current numbers shown at the bottom of the document window.) The options in the menu are disabled, because the document window is currently maximized within the application window.

```
763 x 405
              592w
              536 x 196   (640 x 460, Default)
              600 x 300   (640 x 460, Maximized)
              760 x 420   (800 x 600, Maximized)
              795 x 470   (832 x 624, Maximized)
              955 x 600   (1024 x 768, Maximized)
              544 x 378   (WebTV)

              Edit Sizes...
```

Click 🗗

(The Maximize button is in the upper-right corner of the page.) To display the page as a floating document.

3  Activate the Window Size pop-up menu

```
755 x 420   1K / 1 sec
          Window Size
```

(You can click anywhere on the numbers or on the arrow to the right of the numbers.) You'll set the window size for a resolution of 800 x 600 pixels.

Select **760 x 420**

(If necessary.) To set the page size for optimum viewing within a browser window on a monitor that uses a resolution of 800 x 600.

Click 🔲

To maximize the document window.

4  On the Document toolbar, edit the Title box to read **Outlander Spices: Books**

Title: Outlander Spices: Books

To give this page a title. This text will appear in the browser window's title bar.

5  Choose **File**, **Save**

The Save As dialog box appears, because this is a new document that hasn't been saved yet.

Edit the File name box to read **books.html**

File name:        books.html

Click **Save**

6  Verify that books.html appears in the Files panel list

## Inserting and importing text

*Explanation*

You can add text to a Web page by typing in the document window. If the text is in a separate file, you can import the text or copy and paste the text into Dreamweaver.

It's often helpful to use an external file as the source of your Web site text, so you can distribute the file for editing and approval by other members of a development team. When the text is approved and ready, you can copy and paste it into a Web page. You can use Dreamweaver to import text from a text file or from a formatted document, such as a Microsoft Word file.

### Importing text

When you import text from an external document into Dreamweaver, the Insert Document dialog box appears, as shown in Exhibit 2-10, prompting you to specify import and formatting options.

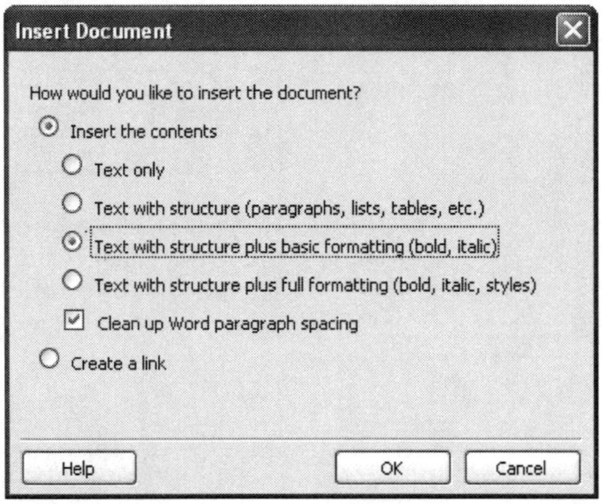

*Exhibit 2-10: The Insert Document dialog box*

The options in the Insert Document dialog box are described in the following table.

| Option | Description |
|---|---|
| Insert the contents; Create a link | Define how the text file is imported, according to your selection of one of these two options. If you insert the contents, the text is copied to the page. If you create a link, a hyperlink to the text file is inserted. If you select "Insert the contents," additional options become available. |
| Text only | Inserts plain text without formatting. |
| Text with structure | Inserts plain text and retains structures such as paragraph breaks, lists, and tables. |
| Text with structure plus basic formatting | Inserts plain or structured text. If any text uses basic formatting, such as bold or italics, Dreamweaver retains this formatting by adding basic HTML tags, where necessary. |
| Text with structure plus full formatting | Inserts plain or structured text and retains all HTML tags and internal CSS styles. |
| Clean up Word paragraph spacing | Removes extra spacing above and below paragraphs in documents imported from Microsoft Word. Available when "Text with structure" is selected. |

**Pasting text**

You can open the text document in the application in which it was created, and then copy and paste the text into Dreamweaver. To control how Dreamweaver formats the pasted text, choose Edit, Paste Special to open the Paste Special dialog box, shown in Exhibit 2-11. The dialog box contains options similar to those in the Insert Document dialog box.

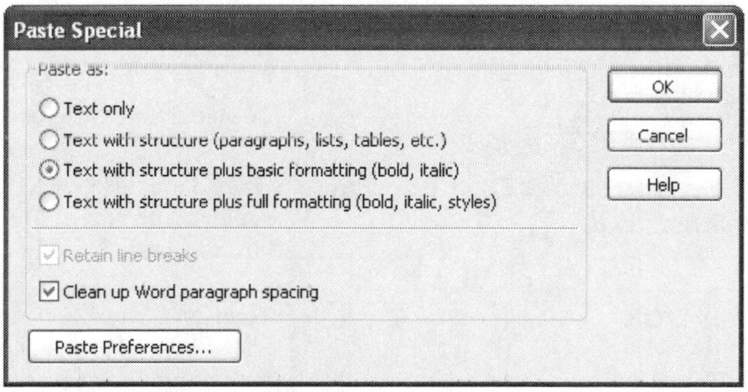

*Exhibit 2-11: The Paste Special dialog box*

*Do it!*

## B-2: Importing text

| Here's how | Here's why |
|---|---|
| 1 From the Files panel, drag **booksinfo1.doc** to the document window | The Insert Document dialog box appears. You'll import text from this Microsoft Word file and then from a simple text file. |
| 2 Verify that **Insert the contents** is selected | You'll insert the contents of the Word document directly into the Web page. |
| Verify that **Text with structure plus basic formatting (bold, italic)** is selected | To import both the text and its basic formatting. |
| Verify that **Clean up Word paragraph spacing** is selected | (If necessary.) To remove unnecessary spaces, carriage returns, and other unwanted characters from the Word document. |
| Click **OK** | To insert the text as specified. Notice that "Outlander Cooking!" appears in italics—the basic formatting was retained. |
| 3 Switch to Code view | Click the Code view button on the Document toolbar. |
| Observe the text | Dreamweaver uses <em> tags to create the italic text that was present in the Word document. |
| Switch to Design view | |
| 4 Place the insertion point as shown | new ingredients and combinat<br>easy-to-follow instructions.&#x7C; |
| | If necessary. |
| Press (← ENTER) | To start a new paragraph. |
| 5 Drag **booksinfo2.txt** below the current text | (From the Files panel.) To add more text from another type of file. The Insert Document dialog box appears. |
| 6 Click **OK** | To insert the text and close the Insert Document dialog box. This is a plain text file with no formatting information in it. |
| 7 Save the page | |

## Page properties

*Explanation*

With the Page Properties dialog box, you can change Dreamweaver's default page properties to customize the appearance of a Web page. You can open the Page Properties dialog box by clicking the Page Properties button in the Property inspector or by choosing Modify, Page Properties.

### Page margins

A *page margin* is the space between a page's content and the edges of the browser window. (Margins may also exist between individual elements.) Browsers apply their own default page margins, most of them applying between 10 and 15 pixels of space on all four sides of the browser window. It's important that you set your own page margins to ensure consistency across various browsers. You can also set your page margins to zero, so that some of your content, such as a navigation bar or header logo, can appear flush with the edge of the browser window. You can then apply margins to large content sections or individual elements to ensure that other content is offset from the browser window's edge and other page elements.

### Background color

By default, Web pages have a white background, but you can apply any background color. To do so, select a color from the Background color box in the Page Properties dialog box. The Background color box displays a *color picker*—a palette with a set of color swatches, as shown in Exhibit 2-12. By default, the color picker displays the Web Safe Colors, a standard set of 216 colors supported consistently across various operating systems.

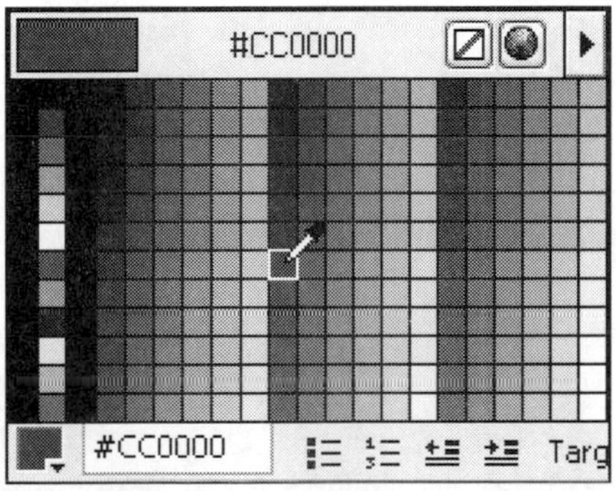

*Exhibit 2-12: The color picker display of color swatches*

### Hexadecimal values

When you select a color swatch in the color picker, the six digit hexadecimal code for the color appears at the bottom, as shown in Exhibit 2-12.

Computer monitors use combinations of red, green, and blue to create the colors you see, and a hexadecimal scheme is used to identify various combinations of those colors: the first two characters represent the intensity of red, the next two of green, and the last two of blue. Hex notation uses the scale 0123456789ABCDEF, with 0 representing almost no color and F representing 15 times the intensity of 0. Hexadecimal values always start with the pound sign (#).

A computer monitor uses light to display color. When you add the colors together, you get white; and the absence of all colors is black, as if you've turned the light off. So, for example, #000000 (the lowest level of red, green, and blue) is black, and #FFFFFF is white. To get yellow, you would add red and green, but no blue, so the hex code would be #FFFF00.

*Do it!*

### B-3: Setting page properties

| Here's how | Here's why |
|---|---|
| 1  In the Property inspector, click **Page Properties...** | To open the Page Properties dialog box. You'll use this to change the appearance of the page. |
| 2  Click the Background color box | A color picker appears. The pointer changes to an eyedropper. |
| Click as shown | #FFFFCC  In the bottom-right corner. |
| 3  In the Left margin box, enter **0** | To give the page a left margin of zero pixels. |
| 4  In the three other margin boxes, enter **0** | To set the margin to zero on all four sides of the page. |
| 5  Click **OK** | To apply the changes and close the Page Properties dialog box. Notice that there's no space between the edges of the document window and the content. |
| 6  Switch to Code view | Dreamweaver embeds a style sheet in the head section of the page to control the page properties that you set. |
| Switch to Design view | |
| 7  Save the page | |

### Text color

*Explanation*

By default, all text is black. You can change the color of selected text on a page, or you can set a default color for all text on a page. You might want to do this if your Web site uses a colored background that makes black text difficult to read, or just to establish a complementary color scheme. Whenever you apply text colors and background colors, you should always make sure that there's sufficient contrast between the text color and background color to allow for easy reading. Insufficient contrast can strain the eyes and make reading the content difficult.

To set the default color for all text on the page:

1   In the Property inspector, click Page Properties to open the Page Properties dialog box.

2   In the Category list, select Appearance, if necessary.

3   Click the text color box.

4   Select a color swatch.

5   Click OK.

To change the color of selected text:

1   Select the text.

2   In the Property inspector, click the color picker.

3   Select a color.

## B-4:    Setting a default text color

| Here's how | Here's why |
|---|---|
| 1 Open the Page Properties dialog box | (In the Property inspector, click Page Properties.) You'll change the default text color for the page. |
| 2 Click the text color box | To open the color picker. |
| Click as shown | |
| | To select a dark green color. |
| 3 Click **OK** | To close the dialog box. All the text in the document is now dark green. |
| 4 In the first paragraph, select **great** | |
| | You'll change the color of this word. |
| 5 In the Property inspector, click the text color box | |
| | To open the color picker. |
| Select a light green color | |
| | To apply this color to the selected text. |
| 6 Click the page | To deselect the text. The green text on the yellow background is difficult to read. |
| 7 Apply a darker color to the word **great** | Select the text. Then, in the Property inspector, click the color picker and select a darker color. |

8  In the Document toolbar, click ⊙▾

(The Preview/Debug in browser button) A dropdown list appears.

Select **Preview in IExplore**

To view the page in Internet Explorer. The Adobe Dreamweaver CS3 dialog box appears.

Click **Yes**

To save the page in its current state. The page appears in the default browser.

9  Close the browser

Close the page

# Unit summary: Web sites and pages

**Topic A**    In this topic, you learned some basic concepts for planning a Web site, and you learned how to define a Web site. You also learned how to use the **Files panel** to display your site files and folders, along with the **Assets panel** to view your site's assets, including images and colors.

**Topic B**    In this topic, you learned how to create and title Web pages. You learned how to **import text** from external documents and to set **page margins**. Finally, you learned how to set a **default text color** and **background color**.

## Independent practice activity

In this activity, you'll define a new Web site, create a Web page, and add text to it. Then you'll set page margins.

1  Choose **Site, New Site** to open the Site Definition Wizard.

2  Enter **Outlander Practice** as the site name, and **http://www.outlanderspices.com** for the site URL.

3  Click **Next** and then click **Next** again.

4  On the Editing Files, Part 3 page, navigate to the Practice folder in the current unit folder.

5  On the Sharing files page, choose **None** as the server connection, and click **Next**.

6  Click **Done** to complete the wizard.

7  Create a new blank page and title it **Outlander Spices: Videos**. (*Hint:* Choose File, New to create the new page. Select Blank Page, and click **Create**.)

8  Save the page as **videos.html** in the Outlander Spices folder, in the Practice subfolder.

9  Import text from videosinfo.doc into videos.html. (*Hint*: Drag the Microsoft Word file from the Files panel to the document window. Insert the text with structure plus basic formatting.)

10  Set all four page margins to **20**. (*Hint*: In the Property inspector, click Page Properties.)

11  Give the page a light background color of your choice. (*Hint:* In the Page Properties dialog box, click the Background color swatch.)

12  Set a new default text color of your choice. (*Hint:* In the Page Properties dialog box, click the Text color swatch.)

13  Make the text **spice up your recipes** appear in a different color from the rest of the text.

14  Save and close videos.html.

## Review questions

1 Which are things to consider when you start to plan a site? [Choose all that apply.]

   A Who your target audience is.

   B How you want the site to look.

   C How best to structure your pages and content.

   D How big you can make the site.

2 Which panel keeps track of site components, such as images or multimedia files?

   A Reference panel

   B Assets panel

   C Snippets panel

   D History panel

3 The Assets panel displays which of the following? [Choose all that apply.]

   A The images in the Web site.

   B The folders in the Web site.

   C The colors in use in the Web site.

   D The HTML files that comprise the Web site.

   E The script files in the Web site.

4 How can you add a title to a page?

   A Double-click the page, then enter the title in the Page Title dialog box.

   B Choose Insert, Page Title, then enter the title in the Page Title dialog box.

   C Enter the title in the Page Title box in the Property inspector.

   D Enter the title in the Title box on the Document toolbar.

5 How can you change the dimensions of the document window?

   A Choose Views, Switch Views, and select a page dimension from the list.

   B Float the document window, and then select a page dimension from the Window Size dropdown menu.

   C Select a page dimension from the Window Size dropdown menu.

   D Float the document window, then choose Views, Switch Views, and select a page dimension from the menu.

6   What's a starter page?

   A   A pre-built page design that you can modify, using your own content.

   B   The home page in a site.

   C   A new HTML page before you add any content to it.

   D   .The default page that opens when you open a site.

7   How can you open the Preferences dialog box?

   A   Double-click the page.

   B   Choose Edit, Preferences.

   C   In the Property inspector, click the Page Properties button.

   D   Choose Window, Preferences.

8   Which options are available in the Paste Special dialog box? [Choose all that apply.]

   A   Text with structure (paragraphs, lists, tables, etc.)

   B   Text with structure plus basic formatting (bold, italic)

   C   Text only

   D   Text in RTF format

9   How can you open the Page Properties dialog box? [Choose all that apply.]

   A   Double-click the page.

   B   In the Property inspector, click the Page Properties button.

   C   Ctrl-click the page.

   D   Choose Modify, Page Properties.

10   How can you change the default text color on a page?

   A   Open the Page Properties dialog box. In the Category list, select Appearance, then click the text color box and select a color.

   B   Select some text on the page, then click the text color box in the Property inspector and select a color.

   C   Double-click the page, then click the text color box and select a color.

   D   Choose Text, Text Color, then select a color.

# Unit 3

## Text formatting

**Unit time: 70 minutes**

Complete this unit, and you'll know how to:

**A** Convert line breaks to paragraph breaks and insert special characters.

**B** Define a basic page structure and create and modify lists.

**C** Create CSS style sheets, apply styles to text, and create class styles and pseudo-element styles.

# Topic A: Text basics

This topic covers the following Adobe ACE exam objectives for Dreamweaver CS3.

| # | Objective |
|---|-----------|
| **2.11** | Given a scenario, set development Preferences. |
| **3.2** | Use Find and Replace including support for regular expressions. |
| **3.12** | List and describe the options available for formatting the structure of a document. (Options include: paragraph breaks, line breaks, non-breaking spaces, tables.) |
| **3.17** | Given a coding tool or feature, describe the purpose of or how to use that tool or feature. (Tools or features include: Code and Design View, Code Collapse, Code Navigation, Code Hinting, Coding Context Menu option.) |

## Line breaks and paragraph breaks

*Explanation*

When you type text in Dreamweaver, it appears on the page starting at the insertion point. You can differentiate how text flows using line or paragraph breaks. However, some characters can't be entered into an HTML document by typing them. Special characters, such as the copyright or trademark symbols, must be entered as HTML codes.

In a word processor, you use line breaks and paragraph breaks to mark the ends of lines and paragraphs. A line break forces text to begin on a new line but within the same paragraph. A paragraph break begins a new line and marks the end of a paragraph. These codes are usually hidden in a word-processing document, but they can be displayed, if necessary, as shown in Exhibit 3-1. Dreamweaver uses its own visual cues to indicate line breaks and paragraph breaks.

This·sentence·ends·in·a·line·break. ↵
This·second·sentence·ends·in·a·line·break. ↵
All·three·lines·are·part·of·the·same·paragraph. ¶

This·sentence·ends·in·a·paragraph·break. ¶
This·second·sentence·is·a·separate·paragraph. ¶

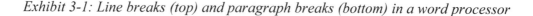

*Exhibit 3-1: Line breaks (top) and paragraph breaks (bottom) in a word processor*

### Line and paragraph breaks in Dreamweaver

Many of Dreamweaver's text formatting options are paragraph-based, which means that text formatting is applied to an entire paragraph. If you copy text from a word processor into a Dreamweaver page, line breaks and paragraph breaks are converted automatically to HTML tags. To apply formatting to individual paragraphs, you must define them as separate paragraphs. To display line breaks in the document window, open the Preferences dialog box, select the Invisible Elements category, check Line Breaks, and click OK.

**Find and Replace**

If you need to convert multiple instances of a particular word, phrase, or even code (such as a line break) to another code, such as a paragraph break, you can use the Find and Replace window. Doing so can help you save time and prevent omissions. Regular expressions can define specific patterns of text strings, which can be helpful in searching the source code in a large and complex HTML file. Dreamweaver provides dozens of special characters that you can use in regular expressions. The following table lists some frequently used characters.

| Character | Finds | Search example |
|---|---|---|
| \| | Any instance of the string on either side of the character | "Green\|blue" returns any instance of "green" or "blue" |
| \d | Any numeral | Any character 0 through 9 |
| \D | Any non-numeric character | Letters, punctuation, and special characters |
| \W | Any non-alphanumeric character | Punctuation and special characters |

To use Find and Replace:

1   Choose Edit, Find and Replace. (Or press Ctrl + F.) The Find and Replace dialog box opens.
2   From the Search list, select Source Code, or Text.
3   Enter the text string to be found in the Find box.
4   Enter the replacement in the Replace box, as shown in Exhibit 3-2.
5   Click Find to search, or Replace to search and replace.
6   Click Close to close the dialog box.

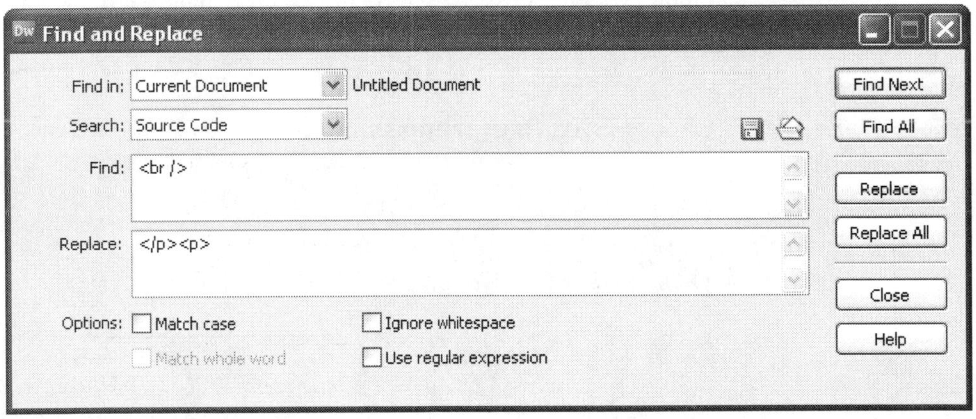

*Exhibit 3-2: The Find and Replace dialog box*

*Do it!*

## A-1:   Changing line breaks to paragraph breaks

| Here's how | Here's why |
|---|---|
| 1  Choose **Site, New Site...** | The Site Definition Wizard appears. You'll create a Web site. |
| 2  For the site name, enter **Outlander -Text** | |
|    For the HTTP address, enter **http://www.outlanderspices.com** | |
|    Click **Next** | |
|    Click **Next** | The Editing Files, Part 3 screen appears. |
| 3  Click ▢ | To open the "Choose local root folder for Outlander Spices Text" dialog box. |
|    Browse to the current unit folder | |
|    Open the Outlander Spices folder, and click **Select** | |
|    Click **Next** | The Sharing Files screen appears. |
| 4  From the top list, select **None** | |
|    Click **Next** | |
| 5  Click **Done** | To create the site. |
| 6  Open aboutus.html | (From the Files panel.) You'll separate headings from text with paragraph breaks, so that you can apply paragraph formatting. |
| 7  Choose **Edit, Preferences...** | To open the Preferences dialog box. You'll show line breaks to make it easier to work with the text. |
|    In the Category list, select **Invisible Elements** | |
|    Check **Line breaks** | ☑ Line breaks |
|    Click **OK** | Line breaks now appear in the document window. |

| | | | |
|---|---|---|---|
| 8 | Locate the first line break | | |

All Spiced Up
Outlander Spices oper
world and select gourr

(In Design view.) This text is on a separate line but is still part of the paragraph that follows it. If you want the heading and the text that follows it to have different styles, you need to make them separate paragraphs.

9 Select **All Spiced Up**, as shown

All Spiced Up
Outlander Spices ope
world and select gour

10 Click [ Split ]

To split the document window into Code view and Design view. The selection in Design view is also highlighted in Code view.

In Code view, observe the HTML tags at the beginning and end of the text

```
<body>
<p><img src="images/logo
<p>All Spiced Up<br />
Outlander Spices opened
```

The line begins with a paragraph tag and ends with a line break tag. The `<p>` tag indicates the start of a paragraph, and the `<br />` tag is the line break.

11 In Design view, click the line break icon

To select it. The code for the line break is selected in Code view. You'll replace this line break with a paragraph break.

Press ( DELETE )

In Design view, the line break icon is deleted. In Code view, the `<br />` tag is deleted.

Press ( ↵ ENTER )

To replace the line break with a paragraph break.

12 Observe the code

```
<p>All Spiced Up</p>
<p> Outlander Spices open
t quality spices from all
```

A closing paragraph tag now marks the end of the text, "All Spiced Up," and an opening paragraph tag now marks the beginning of the next line of text.

13 Observe Design view

All Spiced Up

Outlander Spices op

The line break icon is gone, and a larger space separates the title from the text below it.

| | |
|---|---|
| 14 Choose **Edit**, **Find and Replace...** | To open the Find and Replace dialog box. You'll replace the remaining line break tags with paragraph tags. |
| In the Search list, select **Source Code** | To search the code. |
| 15 In the Find box, enter **\<br /\>** | You'll look for all instances of the line break tag. |
| In the Replace box, type **\</p\>** | |
| Press (SHIFT) + (↵ ENTER) | To create a soft return in the Replace box. Doing this allows the starting paragraph tag to appear on a new line in the code. |
| Type **\<p\>** | |
| 16 Click **Find Next** | To find the next occurrence of the \<br /\> tag. |
| 17 Click **Replace** | To replace the \<br /\> tag with a closing paragraph tag and a starting paragraph tag. The Property inspector indicates that you have made changes to the code. |
| Click in Design view | To force Design view to refresh. The "About our spices" heading converts to a separate paragraph. |
| Click **Replace All** | To replace the remaining line break tags with paragraph tags. The Property inspector indicates that you've made changes to the code, and the Results panel group appears below the Property inspector. |
| 18 Observe the Results panel group | The Search tab displays a list of the replacements made. |
| Right-click the Results tab and select **Close panel group** | |
| | To close the Results panel group. |
| 19 Save the page | |

## Special characters

*Explanation*

Some characters that you might need in your content aren't included on a computer keyboard, such as the copyright symbol (©) or specific language characters, such as the umlaut (ü). You can insert these special characters in a Web page by using their corresponding character entities, which are HTML codes that begin with an ampersand (&) and end with a semicolon. The following table lists some common examples.

| Character | Symbol | HTML code |
|---|---|---|
| Copyright | © | &copy; |
| Registered trademark | ® | &reg; |
| Degree | ° | &deg; |

### Inserting special characters

The codes required for these special characters aren't always intuitive or easy to remember, so Dreamweaver provides a list of hints. To insert a special character:

1  In Code view, place the insertion point where you want the special character to appear.
2  Type & (ampersand). A list of hints for special characters appears.
3  Scroll through the list to find the desired character. The HTML code for the character appears in the right column in black, and the character appears in the left column in blue.
4  Select a character from the list.

### Adding spaces

In HTML, you can't add more than one standard space between words. To insert more than one space, you can use the *non-breaking space* character ( ). This special character adds a single space without forcing a line break.

*Do it!*

## A-2: Inserting special characters and spaces

| Here's how | Here's why |
|---|---|
| 1 Switch to Code view | |
| Scroll to the bottom of the page | You'll replace the word "Copyright" with the copyright symbol. |
| Select **Copyright**, as shown | ```<p>Our team of ded Outlander Spices r <p>Copyright Outla </body> </html>``` |
| | Double-click it, or drag to select it. |
| 2 Type **&** | A list appears, with a variety of special characters. |
| 3 Type **co** | ```Outlander Spices remai <p>&co Outlander Spice </body>ç &ccedil; </html>. &cedil; ¢ &cent; ^ &circ; © &copy; ¤ &curren; ° &deg; ÷ &divide; É &Eacute; é &eacute;``` |
| | Dreamweaver highlights the copyright symbol. |
| 4 Press ↵ ENTER | To insert the copyright symbol. |
| 5 Switch to Design view | |
| Verify the results | © Outlander Spices <br> `<body> <p>` |
| | (Scroll down, if necessary.) The copyright symbol appears. |
| 6 In Code view, place the insertion point before **All**, as shown | `-2007. |All rights reserved` |
| | You'll insert spaces after the copyright notice. |
| Press SPACEBAR four times | `-2007.    |All rights reserved` |
| | To insert four spaces in the HTML code. |
| 7 Switch to Design view | The ordinary spaces entered in the HTML code don't have any effect. |

8  Switch to Code view and delete the four spaces

9  Type **&**

To display the list of special characters. You'll insert non-breaking spaces.

Type **nb**

To select nbsp; from the list.

Press ⏎ ENTER

To insert a non-breaking space.

10  Insert three more non-breaking spaces, as shown

```
t leader in quality spices.</p>
07.     All
```

11  Switch to Design view

```
© Outlander Spices 2005-2007.    All right
<body> <p>
```

The four non-breaking spaces create additional space.

12  Save the page

# Topic B: Structure

*Explanation*
Headings, paragraphs, and other structural elements allow you to organize a Web page into a logical hierarchy, which can make your pages more searchable, easier to read, and easier for other developers to modify. A well-designed page structure can also make it easier to design and arrange your page content and make your content accessible to users with alternative browsing devices.

## Document structure

If you want to create a heading for a page or a section, you should define the text as a heading and not simply change the appearance of the text to *resemble* a heading. The heading level you choose should logically reflect the nature of the content.

For example, if you have a heading that serves as the top-level heading on a page, you should define it as Heading 1. To do so, select the text, and in the Property inspector, select Heading 1 from the Format list. In the code, this command assigns the `<h1>` tag to the text. You can also manually enclose the text in an `<h1>` tag, if you prefer to work in Code view, when you build your document structure. You can also choose Text, Paragraph Format, and then select a heading.

Using meaningful and logical structures—such as Heading 1 for top-level headings and Heading 2 for subheadings—creates consistency on your pages, saves you time and effort when you later update your pages, and allows your pages to be indexed by search engines more efficiently. Headings can also improve the readability of a page. A page that's neatly structured into sections also helps readers find what they're looking for.

### Headings and paragraphs

When you're creating a document that requires multiple headings and subheadings, think of it as a traditional outline. HTML includes six headings that you can use to structure your documents. The tags for these headings are `<h1>` through `<h6>`. Each has its own default formatting. All headings appear bold by default, and they appear in different font sizes. The `<h1>` tag applies the largest default font size, and the `<h6>` applies the smallest default font size. For example, if you're creating a page intended to deliver company news, an effective structure might look something like this:

```
<h1>Company News</h1>
<p>First paragraph of Company News...</p>
<p>Second paragraph of Company News...</p>
<h2>Subheading of Company News</h2>
<p>First paragraph of sub-topic...</p>
```

When you're creating your document structure, don't focus on how each element appears in the browser; you can change that later using CSS. Instead, think about how best to define the content you're working with, creating a logical arrangement of headings, paragraphs, and lists.

*Do it!*

**B-1:   Creating headings**

| Here's how | Here's why |
|---|---|
| 1 Click the text "All Spiced Up" | (At the top of the page.) To place the insertion point in this line. Paragraph formatting always applies to an entire paragraph. |
| In the Property inspector, from the Format list, select **Heading 1** | To convert the text to a level one heading. You can also choose Text, Paragraph Format, Heading 1. |
| 2 In Code view, observe the heading code | The text is now enclosed in `<h1>` tags to define it properly as a level one heading. |
| Switch to Design view | |
| 3 Convert "About our spices" to a level two heading | Click the text, and then choose Heading 2 from the Format list in the Property inspector. |
| 4 Convert the next "About our…" line to a level two heading | |
| 5 Convert "Expansion project" to a level one heading | |
| 6 Save and close aboutus.html | |

## Lists

*Explanation*

HTML provides three list types: unordered lists, ordered lists, and definition lists. In an unordered list, a bullet, circle, square, or other icon precedes each list item. By default, an unordered list uses bullets, as shown in Exhibit 3-3. Use an unordered list when the sequence of the list items isn't important or relevant.

```
Our most popular spices include:

  • Bay leaf
  • Cinnamon
  • Coriander
  • Nutmeg
  • Turmeric
```

*Exhibit 3-3: An example of an unordered list*

In an ordered list, a number or letter indicates each item's order in the list, as shown in Exhibit 3-4. By default, ordered lists are numbered 1, 2, 3, and so on. You can also choose Alphabet Large (A, B, C), Alphabet Small (a, b, c), Roman Large (I, II, III), or Roman Small (i, ii, iii). Use an ordered list when the sequence of items is important.

```
Directions:

  1. Whisk the yogurt with the paste. Mix well.
  2. Heat the oil, reduce the heat, and then add onions, ginger and garlic.
  3. Add the potatoes and fry until golden brown.
  4. Add the yogurt paste.
  5. Cook for 5 minutes.
  6. Add ¾ cup of warm water. Bring to a boil and reduce heat.
  7. Cook until the potatoes are tender and the gravy is thick.
```

*Exhibit 3-4: An example of an ordered list*

You can also create a definition list, which doesn't use bullets or numbers. A definition list is for terms and their definitions and is often used in glossaries, "frequently asked questions" (FAQs) pages, and similar contexts. As shown in Exhibit 3-5, each definition is indented beneath its term. This indentation is the only default formatting that browsers apply to a definition list.

```
Cinnamon
      Cinnamon is one of our most popular spices, due to its sweet flavor and
      prominent role in baked goods and candies. Cinnamon is also wonderful in
      stews and sauces.
Nutmeg
      Nutmeg comes from the seed of a tropical tree. It has a sweet, rich and
      aromatic flavor that complements meats, vegetables, tomato sauces, and
      baked goods.
```

*Exhibit 3-5: An example of a definition list*

**Nested lists**

A *nested list* is a list inside another list. For example, a step in a list of instructions might require its own list of sub-steps. To make a nested list, select the content that you want to turn into a nested list, and click Text Indent in the Property inspector.

*Do it!*

## B-2:  Creating lists

| Here's how | Here's why |
|---|---|
| 1  Open recipes.html | (Double-click the file in the Files panel.) You'll convert ordinary text to ordered and unordered lists. |
| 2  Select all paragraphs between the "Ingredients" and "Directions" subheadings, as shown | Potatoes, washed and quartered: 2 ½ cups<br><br>Oil: ½ cup<br><br>Onions chopped: ½ cup<br><br>Yogurt: ½ cup<br><br>**Dry roast and grind to a paste with a little water:**<br><br>Almonds, blanched peeled and sliced: 3 tbsp<br><br>Outlander Spices Cinnamon powder: 1 ½ tsp<br><br>Outlander Spices Nutmeg powder: 1 ½ tsp<br><br>Outlander Spices Coriander powder: 1 ½ tsp<br><br>Outlander Spices Red chili powder: 3 tsp<br><br>Garlic paste: 2 tsp<br><br>Ginger paste: 2 tsp<br><br>You'll convert these paragraphs to a single, unordered list. |

3 In the Property inspector, click [≣]

(The Unordered List button.) To change the selected text to an unordered list.

Click anywhere on the page

Ingredients

- Potatoes, washed and quartered: 2 ½ cups
- Oil: ½ cup
- Onions chopped: ½ cup
- Yogurt: ½ cup
- **Dry roast and grind to a paste** [BR]
  **with a little water:**
- Almonds, blanched peeled and sliced: 3 tbsp
- Outlander Spices Cinnamon powder: 1 ½ tsp
- Outlander Spices Nutmeg powder: 1 ½ tsp
- Outlander Spices Coriander powder: 1 ½ tsp
- Outlander Spices Red chili powder: 3 tsp
- Garlic paste: 2 tsp
- Ginger paste: 2 tsp

Directions:

To deselect the paragraphs. The paragraphs are converted to items in an unordered list, which is a more appropriate structure for this particular content.

4 Switch to Code view

Observe the code for the unordered list

```
15        <ul>
16            <li>Potatoes, washed a
17            <li>Oil: &frac12; cup<
18            <li>Onions chopped: &fr
19            <li>Yogurt: &frac12; cu
20            <li><strong>Dry roast
21                with a little
22            <li>Almonds, blanched
23            <li>Outlander Spices C
24            <li>Outlander Spices N
25            <li>Outlander Spices C
26            <li>Outlander Spices R
27            <li>Garlic paste: 2 ts
28            <li>Ginger paste: 2 ts
29        </ul>
```

Each item in the list is defined by the `<li>` tag, and every list item is nested inside the `<ul>` tag, the unordered list tag.

Switch to Design view

5 Select the paragraphs under "Directions," as shown

Whisk the yogurt with the roasted paste. M

Heat the oil: reduce the heat, add onions, gi

Add the potatoes and fry until golden brown
water. Bring to a boil, reduce heat, and coo
`<body>`

You'll convert these paragraphs into an ordered list.

6  In the Property inspector, click ☷ | (The Ordered List button.) To convert the text to an ordered list.

   Deselect the text

> Directions:
>
> 1. Whisk the yogurt with the roasted pa
> 2. Heat the oil: reduce the heat, add oni
> 3. Add the potatoes and fry until golder warm water. Bring to a boil, reduce l

(Click the anywhere on the page.) The text is now an ordered list with three sequential steps.

7  Select all list items from "Almonds" to "Red chili powder," as shown

> • **Dry roast and grind to a paste with a little water:**
> • Almonds, blanched peeled and sl
> • Outlander Spices Cinnamon pow
> • Outlander Spices Nutmeg powde
> • Outlander Spices Coriander pow
> • Outlander Spices Red chili powd
> • Garlic paste: 2 tsp

You'll indent these list items to create a nested list.

8  In the Property inspector, click ⊞

(The Text Indent button.) To indent this part of the list, creating a nested list. The items are indented and have a different default bullet style. You can change the bullet type for a list.

9  Choose **Text**, **List**, **Properties** | To open the List Properties dialog box.

   From the Style list, select **Square** | To change the bullets for the nested list to squares.

   Click **OK**

> with a little water:
> ▪ Almonds, blanched peeled
> ▪ Outlander Spices Cinnamo
> ▪ Outlander Spices Nutmeg
> ▪ Outlander Spices Coriand
> ▪ Outlander Spices Red chili

To apply the new bullet style to the selected items.

10  Deselect the text

11  Save and close recipes.html

# Topic C: Cascading Style Sheets

This topic covers the following Adobe ACE exam objectives for Dreamweaver CS3.

| # | Objective |
|---|-----------|
| 1.2 | Describe the difference between CSS classes and IDs. |
| 2.9 | Create pages by using CSS starter pages. |
| 3.4 | Create and maintain Cascading Style Sheets (CSS.) |

## Format text using CSS

*Explanation*

Cascading Style Sheets (CSS) is the standard style language for the Web, and it allows you to control how HTML elements appear in a browser. For example, you can use CSS to define how `<h1>` elements look on all the pages in your site or on a particular page.

You can change the default styles that browsers apply to certain HTML elements. For example, by default, all browsers make text inside an `<h1>` tag large and bold. You can control elements of page design and layout, such as margins, spacing, colors, and borders. What makes CSS especially powerful is that you can link multiple pages to a style sheet, so that you can change any number of Web pages by simply changing style rules once.

This can save a lot of time when you need to update a site's design, and it ensures a consistent appearance throughout a site. CSS also allows you to create leaner, more efficient pages, because the style rules appear only once in a style sheet, rather than repeating in every page.

## Internal and external style sheets

You can define and apply styles for HTML elements by using external or internal style sheets or both.

- **External style sheet:** You define styles in a text file saved with a .css extension. Then, link your Web pages to the style sheet. Use external style sheets whenever you want the style to be global—when you want the styles to apply to multiple documents in a Web site. When you change a style in an external style sheet, the change is reflected in every page linked to that style sheet.

- **Internal style sheet:** You define styles in the `<head>` section of an individual Web page. Internal styles apply only to the page in which they're defined. Use an internal style sheet when you need a style only for a single page or when you want to override a style in an external style sheet.

**Defining styles**

The most common types of CSS styles are described in the following table.

| Style type | Description |
|---|---|
| Element styles | These styles define the formatting of HTML elements. An element style overrides the default formatting for that HTML element. The syntax to define an element style is:<br><br>`element { property: value; }`<br><br>For example, if you want paragraphs to display in bold type, you'd write:<br><br>`p { font-weight: bold; }` |
| Class styles | Classes enable you to give names to HTML elements. They allow you to define elements and page sections with names that are meaningful to you. For example, you can create a class of the `<p>` element named "important" that applies bold, red text. Any paragraphs that are given that class name will appear with those styles. You can apply class styles to multiple elements on a page. The syntax for a class style is:<br><br>`.className { property: value; }`<br><br>The class name must begin with a period. For example, if you want to create the rule mentioned above, you'd write:<br><br>`.important { font-weight: bold; color: red; }`<br><br>Notice that a semicolon and a space separate each style property. A style rule may contain any number of properties. |
| ID styles | ID styles also allow you to create and name your own elements. However, while a class style can be applied to multiple elements in a page, an ID style can be applied to only one element per page. ID styles are particularly useful for defining major content sections that appear only once on a page, such as a `<div>` element named "navigation" to define a navigation bar, or a `<div>` element named "footer" to define the page footer. The syntax for an ID style is:<br><br>`#IDname { property: value; }`<br><br>The ID name must begin with the pound sign (#). For example:<br><br>`#footer { font-size: 10px; color: gray; }` |

After you create class or ID styles, you need to apply them to the desired page elements. When you do, Dreamweaver applies the class or ID attribute directly to that HTML tag. For example, if you apply the class and ID styles mentioned previously to a paragraph and a div element, the HTML looks like this:

```
<p class="important">Paragraph text</p>

<div id="footer">Page footer text</div>
```

You don't need to learn the details of CSS coding to start applying CSS styles to your Web pages. You can create the styles by using panel groups, dialog boxes, and other methods, and Dreamweaver writes the necessary code for you.

**Starter pages**

One way to begin using CSS immediately is to create Web pages by using starter pages. You can choose a starter page from the Page from Sample category of the New Document dialog box and then modify it to suit your needs. To create a Web page using a starter page:

1 Choose File, New. The New Document dialog box appears.

2 Select Page from Sample.

3 In the Sample Folder list, select Starter Page (Theme).

4 In the Sample Page list, click a page. A preview of the CSS design appears, with a brief description beneath, as shown in Exhibit 3-6.

5 Click Create to create a new HTML page based on the selected starter page.

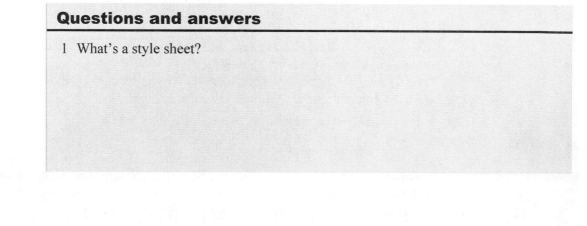

*Exhibit 3-6: CSS starter pages in the New Document dialog box*

*Do it!*

## C-1: Discussing style sheets

### Questions and answers

1 What's a style sheet?

2 What are the two main types of style sheets?

*Internal*

*external*

3 What are the advantages of using an external style sheet?

*global*

4 When might you want to use an internal style sheet?

5 What is CSS?

6 Name three types of styles you can define in a style sheet.

7 If you want the text of *all* level one headings in your site to be blue, what type of style should you use?

8 Describe a scenario in which you'd want to create a class style.

9 Describe a scenario in which you'd want to use ID styles.

## Creating an external style sheet

*Explanation*

To create a new, blank external style sheet:

1 Choose File, New to open the New Document dialog box.
2 Select Blank Page.
3 In the Page Type list, select CSS.
4 Click Create.
5 Save the file and name it with a .css extension. (Preferably in a folder named "styles" inside your site folder.)

You can also use pre-built style sheets and modify them as needed. In the New Document dialog box, select Page from Sample. In the Sample Folder list, select CSS Style Sheet, and then select a sample style sheet.

### The CSS Styles panel

To manage style sheets and apply styles to pages, you can work in the CSS Styles panel, shown in Exhibit 3-7. You can use this panel to link external style sheets to pages, create new styles, and modify existing styles.

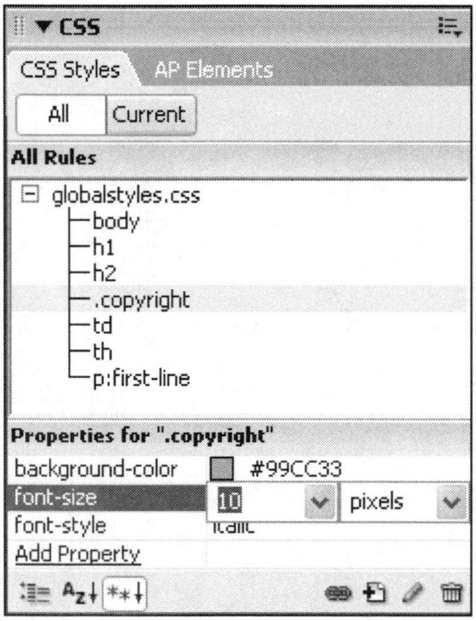

*Exhibit 3-7: The CSS Styles panel*

To link a Web page to an external style sheet:

1 Open the Web page.
2 In the CSS Styles panel, click the Attach Style Sheet button to open the Attach External Style Sheet dialog box.
3 Click Browse to open the Select Style Sheet File dialog box.
4 Navigate to the desired .css file.
5 Click OK to select the file and close the Select Style Sheet File dialog box.
6 Click OK to attach the file and close the Attach External Style Sheet dialog box.

*Do it!*  **C-2:   Creating and attaching an external style sheet**

| Here's how | Here's why |
|---|---|
| 1  Choose **File**, **New...** | To open the New Document dialog box. You'll create a style sheet based on a pre-built style sheet. |
| Select **Page from Sample** | To display the sample pages. |
| In the Sample Folder list, select **CSS Style Sheet** | If necessary. |
| In the Sample Page list, click **Basic: Verdana** | To select a basic style sheet that sets three commonly used tags in the Verdana font. |
| 2  Click **Create** | To create the CSS file. The style sheet opens in the document window. This style sheet has three rules: one for the body element, one for the <td> tag (table cells), and another for the <th> tag (table headers). These styles are all the same, because some browsers don't allow text in tables to inherit styles from the body element. |
| Save the style sheet as **globalstyles.css** in the styles folder | The styles folder is in the Outlander Spices folder, in the current unit folder. |
| Close globalstyles.css | |
| 3  Open aboutus.html | You'll attach the style sheet to this page. The text appears with default styles. |
| 4  Expand the CSS panel group | |
| Click [icon] | (The Attach Style Sheet button.) The Attach External Style Sheet dialog box appears. |
| 5  Click **Browse** | To open the Select Style Sheet File dialog box. |
| Navigate to the styles folder | In the Outlander Spices folder, in the current unit folder. |
| 6  Select **globalstyles.css** | |
| Click **OK** | To attach the style sheet to this page and close the Select Style Sheet File dialog box. |
| Verify that Link is selected | To create a link to this style sheet, rather than embedding its styles directly into aboutus.html. |
| Click **OK** | To close the Attach External Style Sheet dialog box. |
| 7  Observe the text in aboutus.html | The text now appears in the Verdana font. |

| 8 | Switch to Code view | (Click the Show Code view button at the top of the document window.) You'll view the link code. |
| | Locate the link to the style sheet | |
| | | (Around line 9.) The code now includes a link to globalstyles.css. |
| | Switch to Design view | |
| 9 | Save aboutus.html | |

## Text styles

*Explanation*

There are many styles that you can apply to text, including the font (typeface), font size, font weight (degree of boldness), and font style (italics and underlining).

### Font-size units

There are several units of measurement you can use to control font size. The most commonly used are points and pixels. A point is a unit of print measurement that doesn't translate well to the screen. Pixels are a more appropriate choice for display on a Web page. Using pixels typically produces the most consistent results across various browsers and platforms.

### Creating and applying element styles

To create an element style:

1   Open one of the following:
    - A Web page (to define a style that applies to only that page)
    - A style sheet (to define a style in the external style sheet)
2   In the CSS Styles panel, click the New CSS Rule button.
3   In the New CSS Rule dialog box, under Selector type, select Tag.
4   In the Tag list, select the HTML tag (element) to which you'll apply the style.
5   Under Define in, do one of the following:
    - In the list, select a new or existing style sheet file.
    - Select This document only (to create the style in the active document).
6   Click OK.
7   In the CSS Rule Definition dialog box, set the attributes for the style.
8   Click OK.

## C-3: Defining element styles

| Here's how | Here's why |
|---|---|
| 1 In the CSS Styles panel, click [ All ] | (If necessary.) To display the style sheet files. You'll define styles for the `<body>` element and create heading styles. |
| 2 To the left of the style sheet, click as shown | **All Rules**<br>R: globalstyles |
| | (If necessary.) To expand it. There are three styles: body, td, and th. The td rule sets styles for text inside regular table cells, and the th rule sets styles for all table-heading cells. |
| 3 In the style tree, click **body** | ▼ **CSS**<br>CSS Styles  AP El<br>[ All ] [ Current ]<br>**All Rules**<br>⊟ globalstyles.css<br>├─body<br>├─td<br>└─th |
| | You'll define the styles for the body element, setting the default page styles for all pages linked to this style sheet. All elements are inside the body section and, therefore, inherit its styles. |
| Click [ ✎ ] | (The Edit Style button.) To edit the body style. The CSS Rule Definition dialog box appears. |
| From the Size list, select **12**, as shown | Size: [ 12 ▾ ] [ pixels ▾ ] |
| | To set the size of the body text to 12 pixels. The default unit of measurement is pixels. |
| Click **OK** | The body text in aboutus.html changes in accordance with the new font size rule. |
| 4 Click [ ⬦ ] | (The New CSS Rule button.) The New CSS Rule dialog box opens. You'll create a level one heading style. |
| Under Selector Type, select **Tag** | You'll define an element style, meaning that it applies to all instances of a specific HTML tag. |
| In the Tag list, select **h1** | To apply this rule to the `<h1>` element. |

| | | |
|---|---|---|
| 5 | In the Define in list, verify that globalstyles.css is selected | To define this style in the external style sheet, so that it applies to all Web pages that are linked to that style sheet. |
| | Click **OK** | The CSS Rule Definition dialog box appears. |
| 6 | In the Size box, enter **22** | `22 ▾` |
| | | To give all level one headings a font size of 22 pixels. |
| | Click **OK** | To apply the new style. |
| 7 | Create a new CSS rule for the h2 element | Click the New CSS Rule button. In the New CSS Rule dialog box, verify that Tag is selected, choose h2 from the Tag list, and click OK. |
| 8 | In the Size list, enter **18**, and click **OK** | (In the CSS Rule Definition dialog box.) The level two heading in aboutus.html now appears with an 18-pixel font size. |
| 9 | Activate globalstyles.css | (Click the globalstyles.css document tab.) When you edit styles in the style sheet using the CSS Styles panel, it automatically opens the style sheet in the workspace. |
| | Observe that the body rule now includes a font-size property, and that styles have been added for the h1 and h2 tags | |
| 10 | Save the style sheet | |

## Creating class styles

*Explanation*

You can create class styles, or classes, to accompany HTML element styles or to replace them. You can apply classes to any HTML element. For example, let's say you want to apply a special format to one paragraph. If you change the style definition for the <p> tag, the change will affect all paragraphs on pages with that style sheet attached. Instead, you can create a class style, and apply it to only the paragraph(s) where it's needed.

### Class names

Class names must begin with a period. Giving classes meaningful names makes maintenance easier, both for you and for others who might work on the site in the future. For example, a year from now, it'll be easier to figure out where a class is used if it's named ".special" instead of ".class2."

### Creating class styles

As with all CSS styles, you can insert a class style in an internal or external style sheet. To create a class style:

1  Open one of the following:

   - A Web page (to create an internal class style that applies to that page only)
   - A style sheet, or a Web page that's linked to a style sheet (to create a class style in the external style sheet)

2  In the CSS Styles panel, click the New CSS Rule button.

3  In the New CSS Rule dialog box, under Selector type, select Class.

4  In the Name box, type a name that begins with a period (.).

5  Under Define in, do one of the following:

   - In the list, select a new or existing style sheet file.
   - Select This document only (to embed the style in the active document).

6  Click OK.

7  In the CSS Rule Definition dialog box, define the attributes for the style.

8  Click OK.

*Do it!*

### C-4:  Creating class styles

| Here's how | Here's why |
|---|---|
| 1  Activate aboutus.html | You'll create a class style. |
| Create a new CSS rule | (In the CSS Styles panel, click the New CSS Rule button.) The New CSS Rule dialog box opens. |
| Next to Selector Type, select **Class** | To begin creating a new class style. |
| In the Name box, enter **.copyright** | To specify a meaningful and appropriate name. All class names begin with a period. |
| 2  In the Define in list, verify that globalstyles.css is selected | To create this style in the external style sheet, so that the style applies to all Web pages that are linked to the style sheet. |
| Click **OK** | To open the CSS Rule Definition dialog box. |
| 3  In the Size list, enter **11** | To apply a font size of 11 pixels to the .copyright class. |
| From the Style list, select **italic** | To make text defined by the .copyright class italicized. |
| 4  In the Category list, select Block | |
| From the Text align list, select **center** | To center the copyright statement. |
| Click **OK** | Now that you've created the class style, you still need to apply it to the copyright text. |
| 5  In the document window, scroll to the bottom of the page | |
| Click in the copyright text | |
| 6  In the Property inspector, in the Style list, select **copyright** | To apply the new class style to the text. The copyright statement now displays as centered, 11-pixel italic text. |
| 7  Switch to Split view | |
| Observe the code for the copyright text | `<p class="copyright">&copy;` |
| | The class style is applied using the `class` attribute. |
| Switch to Design view | |

8  In the CSS Styles panel, double-click **.copyright**

(In the style tree.) You'll edit the class style.

In the Category list, select **Background**

To specify background attributes for this rule.

9  Click the Background color box

A color palette appears, and the pointer changes to an eyedropper.

Select the green color **#99CC33**

Click **OK**

The copyright text now has a green background.

10  Click the copyright line

(If necessary.) To select it.

In the Property inspector, click [ CSS ]

(The Open CSS Panel button.) To display the Current tab in the CSS Styles panel. If the CSS Panel group is closed, clicking this button opens it.

11  In the CSS Styles panel, in the Summary for Selection list, point to **font-family**

A tooltip appears that describes this property of the copyright line. You can use the CSS Styles panel to review the styles in a given rule quickly and to change the property values.

12  Update the style sheet

## Pseudo-element styles

*Explanation*

You can use pseudo-elements to target specific aspects of an element. Two commonly used pseudo-elements are the first-line pseudo-element and first-letter pseudo-element. The first-line pseudo-element enables you to apply styles to only the first line of a paragraph, and the first-letter pseudo-element enables you to apply styles to only the first letter of a paragraph.

To create a pseudo-element style:

1  Select the Advanced option in the New CSS Rule dialog box, as shown in Exhibit 3-8.

2  In the Selector box, enter the selector you want to associate with the style, such as p (for the paragraph tag) or body (for the body tag), etc. The selector you choose determines the content that's affected by the style.

3  Type a colon, then enter the pseudo-element style you want. For example, to change the first line of text in a paragraph, enter "first-line." To change the first letter in a paragraph, enter "first-letter."

4  Click OK, then enter the style attributes you want in the CSS Rule Definition dialog box.

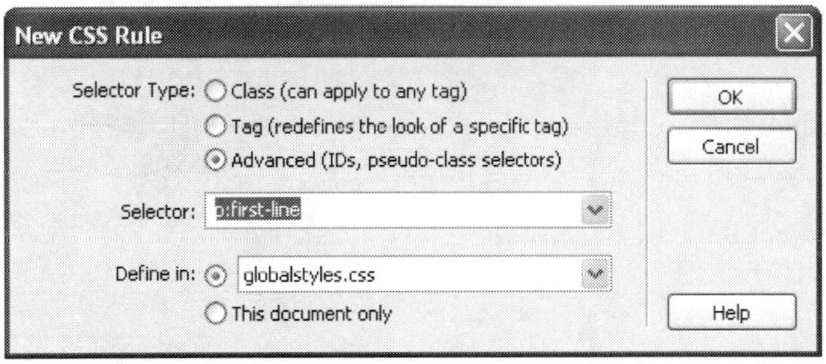

*Exhibit 3-8: Creating a pseudo-element style*

*Do it!*

## C-5: Creating pseudo-element styles

| Here's how | Here's why |
|---|---|
| 1 Activate aboutus.html | You'll create a pseudo-element style. |
| 2 Create a new CSS rule | In the CSS Styles panel, click the New CSS Rule button. |
| 3 Next to Selector Type, select **Advanced** | |
| 4 Click in the Selector list | To select the default selector. |
|    Type **p:first-line** | |
|    Click **OK** | To open the CSS Rule Definition dialog box. |
| 5 From the Weight list, select **bold** | |
|    Click **Apply** | The first line in each paragraph is now bold. (You might have to move the dialog box in order to see the text.) |
| 6 Click the Color box | A color palette appears, and the pointer changes to an eyedropper. |
|    Select the dark green color **#006633** | |
|    Click **OK** | To apply the change. The first lines of all the paragraphs in the aboutus.html page now appear in bold, dark green text. If the widths of the paragraphs change, the amount of styled text changes with it. |
| 7 In the CSS Styles pane, click [ All ] | |
|    Click **p:first-line** | You'll change this style rule. |
|    Click **p:first-line** again | You'll change the selector. |

| | | |
|---|---|---|
| 8 | Type **p:first-letter** | To apply the style only to the first letter of each paragraph. |
| | Double-click **p:first-letter** | You'll edit the styles. |
| | In the Size box, enter **18**, and click **OK** | To update the first-letter pseudo-class style. |
| 9 | Collapse the CSS panel group | |
| 10 | Save and close all open files | |

# Unit summary: Text formatting

**Topic A**       In this topic, you learned how to convert **line breaks** to **paragraph breaks**, and you learned how to insert **special characters** and **non-breaking spaces**.

**Topic B**       In this topic, you learned how to apply **structural tags**, including headings and paragraphs, and you learned that a sound page structure can make it easier to maintain a Web site, as well as design and arrange page content. You also learned how to create **unordered lists**, **ordered lists**, and **nested lists**.

**Topic C**       In this topic, you learned the basics of **Cascading Style Sheets (CSS)**. You learned about the differences between **internal** and **external** style sheets, basic CSS syntax, and the function of element styles, class styles, and ID styles. Then you learned how to create an external style sheet and link documents to it. Finally, you learned how to create and apply **element styles**, **class styles**, and **pseudo-element styles**.

## Independent practice activity

In this activity, you'll attach a style sheet to several pages, create and apply a class style, and define element styles.

1   Choose **Site**, **New Site** to start the Site Definition Wizard.

2   Enter **Outlander Text Practice** as the site name.

3   Enter **http://www.outlanderspices.com** for the site URL.

4   Click **Next** twice.

5   On the Editing Files, Part 3 page, navigate to the Practice folder (in the current unit folder).

6   On the Sharing files page, choose **None** as the server connection, and click **Next**.

7   Click **Done** to complete the wizard.

8   Open index.html.

9   Attach globalstyles.css to index.html. (*Hint*: The style sheet is located in the styles subfolder.)

10  Define the heading, "Awards," as a level two heading.

11  In globalstyles.css, create a class style named **.mission** that makes text bold, italic, and 14 pixels.

12  Apply the new style to the first paragraph in index.html.

13  Open recipes.html and attach globalstyles.css to it.

14  Define a new CSS style for the ul (unordered list) element. (*Hint:* In the New CSS Rule dialog box, select Tag, then select ul from the tag list.)

15  Set the font size for the ul style to 12 pixels. Set the font color to a green, such as #006600. Verify the changes in recipes.html.

16  Define a new CSS style for the ol (ordered list) element.

17  Set the font size for the ol style to 12 pixels. Set the font color to a purple color (such as #660033.) Verify the changes in recipes.html.

18 Save the page and preview it in Internet Explorer. When you're done, close the browser to return to Dreamweaver.

19 Save and close all open files.

## Review questions

1 How can you find and replace a specific section of HTML code?

A Choose Edit, Find and Replace. Select Source Code from the Search list, then enter the code you want to search for and the code with which you want to replace it.

B In Code view, select the code you want to search for. Choose Edit, Replace Code With, and enter the code with which you want to replace it.

C Choose Edit, Find and Replace. Select Text (Advanced) from the Search list, then enter the code you want to search for and the code with which you want to replace it.

D In Code view, select the code you want to search for. In the Coding toolbar, click the Replace button, and enter the code with which you want to replace it.

2 Which tag creates a line break?

A  <p>

B  <em>

C  <br />

D  <line />

3 If you want all the level two headings on your site to have the same formatting, you should:

A  Create an internal element style for the <h2> tag.

B  Create an external element style for the <h2> tag.

C  Create an internal class style.

D  Create an external class style.

4 If you want to create a special type of paragraph with extra large text, and you think you'll need to use the style for multiple paragraphs on a page, it's best to:

A  Create an internal element style for the <p> tag.

B  Create an external element style for the <p> tag.

C  Create an external class style and give it a meaningful name.

D  Create an external ID style and give it a meaningful name.

5  If you want to define a unique section that holds the navigation bar, and you want this element to look the same on every page, it's best to:

A  Create an internal class style and give it a meaningful name, such as "navbar."

B  Create an external class style and give it a meaningful name, such as "navbar."

C  Create an internal ID style and give it a meaningful name, such as "navbar."

D  Create an external ID style and give it a meaningful name, such as "navbar."

6  How can you change the font size in an existing CSS style? (Choose all that apply.)

A  Right-click some text with the style applied, then choose CSS styles, Edit Style. In the dialog box, change the font size and click OK.

B  In the CSS styles panel, select the style, then click the Edit Style button. In the dialog box, change the font size and click OK.

C  Double-click some text with the style applied. In the dialog box, change the font size and click OK.

D  In the CSS styles panel, select the style, then in the Summary for Selection list, point to font-family.

7  What's the correct way to define the first-line pseudo-element for the paragraph selector?

A  p.first-line

B  p:first-line

C  first-line:p

D  first-line.p

# Unit 4
## Tables

**Unit time: 60 minutes**

Complete this unit, and you'll know how to:

**A** Create tables and nested tables.

**B** Format rows and cells, merge cells, and add rows and columns to a table.

**C** Set fixed and variable widths for tables and columns and change cell borders and padding.

**D** Create a layout table to arrange page content.

# Topic A: Create tables

This topic covers the following Adobe ACE exam objectives for Dreamweaver CS3.

| # | Objective |
|---|-----------|
| **2.7** | List and describe the features that Dreamweaver provides for Accessibility Standards/Section 508 compliance. |
| **2.12** | Given a scenario, choose the proper method to lay out a page. |
| **3.8** | Given a method, lay out a page. (Methods include: Table Layout, Layers, Expanded Tables mode.) |
| **3.12** | List and describe the options available for formatting the structure of a document. (Options include: paragraph breaks, line breaks, non-breaking spaces, tables.) |

## Basic tables

*Explanation*

An HTML table is a grid structure of rows and columns that you can use to display tabular data, such as products and prices, or to arrange page elements. Tables can also be nested inside other tables to create more complex grid structures.

### Table structure

Tables are generally meant for data that's best arranged in rows and columns, such as the information shown in Exhibit 4-1. You can also use tables to arrange page content into a layout, but it's generally best to use CSS to achieve layout and style objectives.

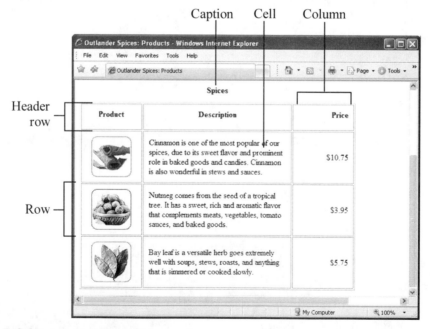

*Exhibit 4-1: A simple table used to arrange content*

### Inserting tables

To insert a table, drag the Table icon from the Common group on the Insert bar to the page. Then, define the basic table settings in the Table dialog box, shown in Exhibit 4-2. You can then use the Property inspector to change table properties as necessary. After you've created a table, you can drag text and images to the cells as needed.

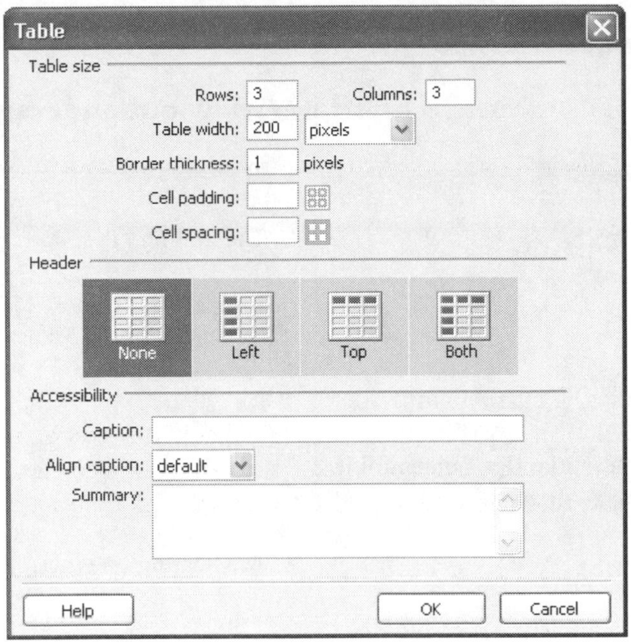

*Exhibit 4-2: The Table dialog box*

The following table describes the options available in the Table dialog box.

| Option | Defines |
|---|---|
| Rows | The number of rows in the table. |
| Columns | The number of columns in the table. |
| Table width | The width of the table, either in pixels or as a percentage of the browser window or of a container, such as an AP div tag. |
| Border thickness | The width of the cell borders. |
| Cell padding | The amount of space between a cell's contents and the cell's border. |
| Cell spacing | The amount of space between adjacent cells. |
| Header | The left column, the top row, or both, used as a heading. |
| Caption | A title that describes the table. |
| Align caption | The alignment of an optional table caption; you can align it to the top, bottom, left, or right of the table. |
| Summary | A description that can be read by screen readers for the visually impaired. |

## A-1: Creating a table

| Here's how | Here's why |
|---|---|
| 1 Choose **Site**, **New Site...** | To open the Site Definition Wizard. You'll create a Web site. |
| 2 For the site name, enter **Outlander - Tables** | |
| For the HTTP address, enter **http://www.outlanderspices.com** | |
| Click **Next** | |
| Click **Next** | The Editing Files, Part 3 screen appears. |
| 3 Click 🗀 | To open the "Choose local root folder for Outlander Spices Tables" dialog box. |
| 4 Browse to the current unit folder | |
| Open the Outlander Spices folder, and click **Select** | |
| Click **Next** | The Sharing Files screen appears. |
| 5 From the top list, select **None** | |
| Click **Next** | |
| Click **Done** | To create the site. |
| 6 In the Files panel, expand the Site folder | If necessary. |
| 7 Open products.html | You'll create a basic table and add text and images to it. |
| 8 On the Insert bar, activate the Common tab | If necessary. |
| Drag 🖽 to the document window, as shown | |
| | The Table dialog box appears. |
| Edit the Rows box to read **4** | To set the number of table rows to four. |
| Edit the Columns box to read **2** | To set the number of columns to two. |

| | |
|---|---|
| 9  In the list next to the Table width box, verify that pixels is selected | To set the table width in pixels. |
| Edit the Table width box to read **580** | To set the table width to 580 pixels. |
| Under Header, click **Top** | |

To make the top row of the table a header row.

| | |
|---|---|
| 10  In the Caption box, enter **Spices** | To create a table caption. |
| In the Align caption list, verify that **default** is selected | The default alignment for table caption is the top center. |
| 11  In the Summary box, enter **Outlander spices and their descriptions** | To create a summary that describes the content of this table for screen readers used by the visually impaired. |
| Click **OK** | To create the table. At the bottom of the table, the table width is visible. You'll hide the table width information. |
| 12  In the document toolbar, click | To expand the Visual Aid list. |
| Clear **Table Widths** | To hide the table width information. |
| 13  Double-click the caption text | To select it. |
| In the Property inspector, click **B** | To make the caption text bold. |
| 14  In the top row of the left column, type **Product** | To create a heading for this column. By default, the text in this row is bold and centered in each cell, because that's the default style of the `<th>` (table header) element, which defines each cell in this row. You can change these default styles with CSS, if necessary. |
| 15  In the top row of the right column, type **Description** | To create a heading for the right column. |

16  In the Files panel, navigate to the images folder

    (In the Outlander Spices Tables folder, which is in the current unit folder.) You'll add images to the table.

    Drag **cinnamon.jpg** to the cell under "Product"

    The Image Tag Accessibility Attributes dialog box appears.

    In the Alternate text box, enter **Cinnamon image**

    To create alternate text for this image.

    Click **OK**

    To place the image and close the dialog box.

17  Insert **nutmeg.jpg** and **bay leaf.jpg** in the cells below cinnamon.jpg, as shown

Drag the nutmeg image to its cell, specify appropriate alternate text, and click OK. Repeat for the bay leaf image.

18  Open descriptions.txt

    You'll insert text from this file into the table.

    Copy the descriptions of each spice into the corresponding cell in the Description column

    Select each description, copy it, and paste it into the appropriate cell. The cells shift as you add the text.

    Close descriptions.txt

    Delete any line breaks and spaces that appear at the end of each paragraph

If necessary.

19  Save the page and preview it in Internet Explorer

    Close the browser

## Nested tables

*Explanation*    A *nested table* is a table that's inserted into the cell of another table. Nested tables give you more flexibility in arranging content. For example, Exhibit 4-3 shows a nested table in which the outer table contains all the content shown, and the nested table contains text in cells to be used to create a navigation bar. The outer table consists of one column and two rows. The nested table is placed in the second row of the outer table and consists of one row and eight columns.

*Exhibit 4-3: An example of a nested table used for layout purposes*

### Expanded tables mode

Sometimes it's difficult to edit table cells. For example, it can sometimes be difficult to place the insertion point next to an image in a table cell without selecting the image. To make editing tables easier, you can use the expanded tables mode to add cell padding and spacing temporarily and to increase the table's borders. The additional space makes it easier to edit the content or place the insertion point. To view tables in expanded tables mode, select View, Table Mode, Expanded Tables Mode. You can also click the Expanded Tables Mode button in the Layout category of the Insert bar.

*Do it!*    ## A-2:   Creating a nested table

| Here's how | Here's why |
|---|---|
| 1 Drag [icon] to the top-left corner of the page, as shown | 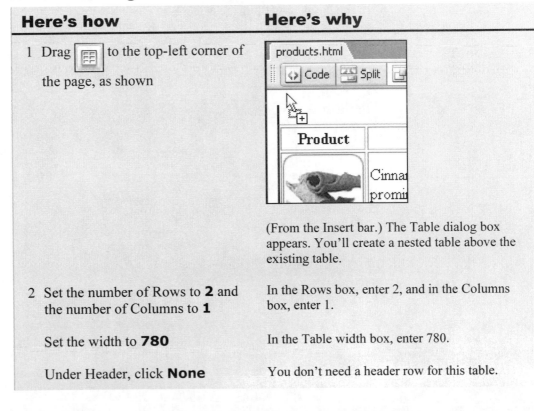 |
| | (From the Insert bar.) The Table dialog box appears. You'll create a nested table above the existing table. |
| 2 Set the number of Rows to **2** and the number of Columns to **1** | In the Rows box, enter 2, and in the Columns box, enter 1. |
| Set the width to **780** | In the Table width box, enter 780. |
| Under Header, click **None** | You don't need a header row for this table. |

3  In the Summary box, enter **Navigation bar**

To create a summary that describes this table. Table summaries provide a context for the table for users with alternative browsers, such as screen readers.

   Click **OK**

4  Insert logo.jpg in the top row

In the Files panel, navigate to the images folder. Drag logo.jpg to the top row. Then, in the Image Tag Accessibility Attributes dialog box, enter alternate text and click OK.

5  Drag [⊞] to the bottom row of the table

To nest another table inside the existing table. The Table dialog box appears.

   Set the number of Rows to **1** and the number of Columns to **8**

   Set the Table width to **780**

If necessary.

   Click **OK**

6  In the eight cells of the nested table, enter the following headings:
   **Home**
   **About Us**
   **Locations**
   **Products**
   **Recipes**
   **Site Search**
   **Order Online**
   **Contact Us**

(As shown in Exhibit 4-3.) These headings will eventually serve as navigation links.

7  Save the page

# Topic B:  Table structure and formatting

This topic covers the following Adobe ACE exam objective for Dreamweaver CS3.

| # | Objective |
|---|-----------|
| 3.12 | List and describe the options available for formatting the structure of a document. (Options include: paragraph breaks, line breaks, non-breaking spaces, tables.) |

*Explanation*

Now that you know how to create tables and add text and images to them, you need to learn to adjust a table's structure and make formatting modifications. To do so, you should be familiar with the various table-related tags and be able to select table components.

## Table formatting

The `<table>` tag defines a table. Within the `<table>` tag, each `<tr>` tag defines a row, and within each row, `<td>` tags define each cell. The number of cells in a row determines the number of columns in the table. For example, Exhibit 4-4 shows the code for a table consisting of two rows—notice the two sets of `<tr>` tags—and three columns. The resulting table is shown on the right.

```
<table>
    <tr>
        <td> </td>
        <td> </td>
        <td> </td>
    </tr>

    <tr>
        <td> </td>
        <td> </td>
        <td> </td>
    </tr>
</table>
```

*Exhibit 4-4: A simple table*

You can select all the cells in a column or row, or select individual cells. You need to select a row, column, or cell before you can set properties for it.

### Selecting table cells

The easiest and fastest way to select an individual cell is to press Ctrl and click the cell. You can also click the cell and choose Edit, Select All, or you can click the cell and then click the rightmost <td> tag in the tag selector at the bottom of the window, as shown in Exhibit 4-5. The tag selector is useful for selecting, editing, or removing tags while you're working in Design view.

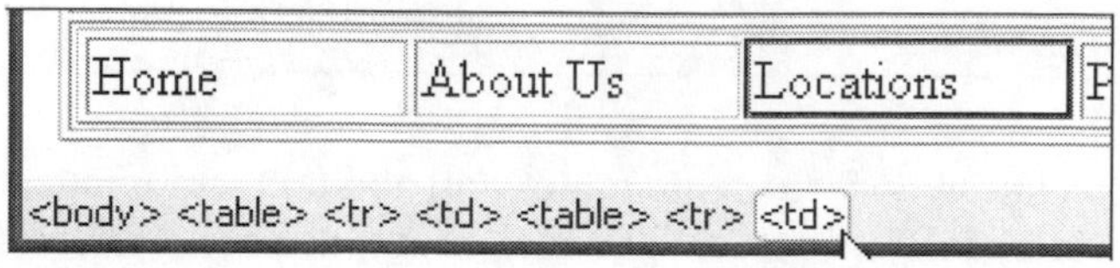

*Exhibit 4-5: Click a cell's tag to select the cell*

### Selecting rows or columns

To select a row or column, do any of the following:

- Point to the left edge of the leftmost cell (for a row) or the top edge of the topmost cell (for a column.) When the pointer changes to a position arrow, click the edge of the cell.
- Click the left cell of a row and drag to the right or click the top cell of a column and drag down.
- (Rows only) Click the cell, and then click the rightmost <tr> tag in the tag selector at the bottom of the window.

### Formatting rows

After you select a row, you can expand the Property inspector to customize the row formatting, as shown in Exhibit 4-6.

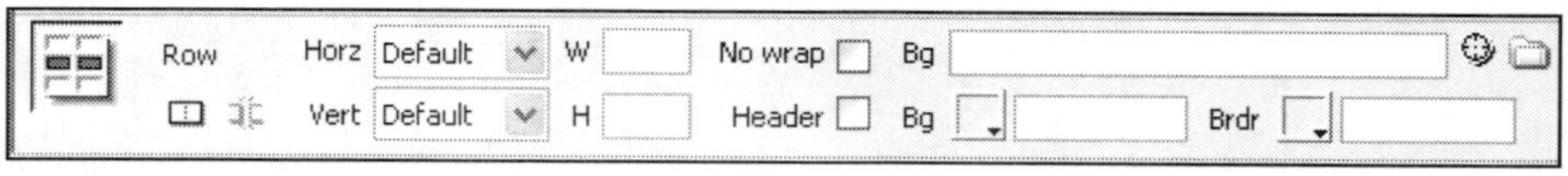

*Exhibit 4-6: The row formatting options of the Property inspector*

Using row formatting options, you can:

- Merge adjacent cells into a single continuous cell.
- Change the horizontal and vertical alignment of objects in the cells in the selected row.
- Change the width and height of the selected row.
- Allow the text in cells to wrap.
- Define the selected row as a table header row.
- Define a background image, background color, and border color.

*Do it!*

**B-1:  Formatting rows**

| Here's how | Here's why |
|---|---|
| 1  In the Products table, point to the left edge of the top-left cell and click once | |
| | (Make sure that the pointer changes to a right-pointing arrow before you click.) To select the row. You'll format this row. |
| 2  In the lower-right corner of the Property inspector, click ▽ | (If necessary.) To expand the Property inspector. |
| In the H box, enter **30** | To set the row height to 30 pixels. |
| In the Vert list, select **Top** | To align the text to the top of the row. |
| 3  Save the page | |

## Modifying cells

*Explanation*

The Property inspector includes the same options for cells as it does for rows, with one exception. The cells in a row can be merged, but when a single cell is selected, you can also split it.

### Cell width

When you change the width of a cell, the entire column might be affected. By default, columns are sized according to the largest cell in the column, which is determined by the size of the content it contains. You can also set specific column widths, in pixels or percentage values.

### Background colors

You can specify a background color for rows, columns, and individual cells. To do so, select the row, column, or cell, and then click the Bg box in the Property inspector to open a color palette. Click a swatch to specify a color.

### Inserting rows and columns

When a single cell is selected, you can add a row of cells above or below it, and you can add a column to the right or left of it.

To insert a row, do any of the following:

- Select a cell and choose Insert, Table Objects, Insert Row Above or Insert Row Below.
- Right-click a cell and choose Table, Insert Row. (The row is inserted above the selected cell.)
- Right-click a cell and choose Table, Insert Rows or Columns. In the dialog box, apply the desired settings and click OK.

To insert a column, do any of the following:

- Select a cell and choose Insert, Table Objects, Insert Column to the Left or Insert Column to the Right.
- Right-click a cell and choose Table, Insert Column. (The column is inserted to the left of the selected cell.)
- Right-click a cell and choose Table, Insert Rows or Columns. In the dialog box, apply the desired settings and click OK.

*Do it!*

## B-2:   Adding columns and rows and formatting cells

| Here's how | Here's why |
|---|---|
| 1 In the Products table, click the cell containing "Description" | To place the insertion point. |
| 2 Choose **Insert**, **Table Objects**, **Insert Column to The Right** | To add a column to the right of the selected cell. |
| 3 Set the cell width to **100** | (In the W box in the Property inspector, enter 100.) Changing the width of the cell affects the entire column. Column widths are set according to the largest cell in the column. |
| 4 In the four new cells, enter **Price**, **$10.75**, **$3.95**, and **$5.75** | To create a column heading and enter the price data for the listed spices. Notice that the top cell in the new column is automatically formatted as a heading, like the other cells in this row. |
| 5 Right-click any cell in the top row and choose **Table**, **Insert Row** | To insert a row at the top of the table. |
| Select the new top row | Point to the left edge of the top-left cell in the Spices table until the pointer turns into an arrow, and then click. |
| Right-click the row and choose **Table**, **Merge Cells** | To merge the top row's cells into a single cell. |
| 6 Click the merged cell | To place the insertion point in the cell. |
| Type **Featured Products** | |

7 In the Property inspector, click the Bg color box, as shown

Select the dark green color **#006600**, as shown

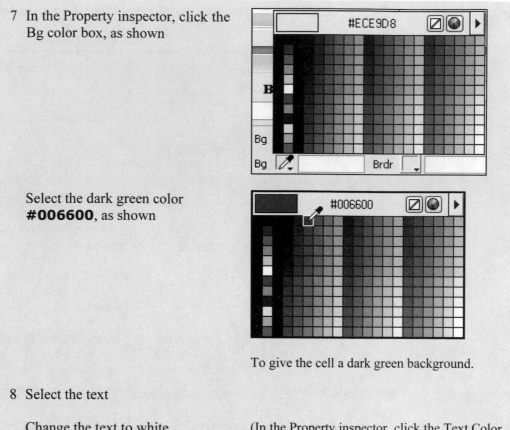

To give the cell a dark green background.

8 Select the text

Change the text to white

(In the Property inspector, click the Text Color box, and select white from the color picker.) To make the text more visible against the dark green background.

9 Save the page

# Topic C:  Column widths and cell properties

*Explanation*

You can further customize the appearance of tables by making column widths fixed or variable, along with specifying their sizes, and by hiding or modifying cell borders.

### Fixed and variable widths for columns and tables

You can set a column's width to a fixed number of pixels or to a percentage of the table width. Similarly, you can set a table's width to either fixed or variable. A variable-width table is sized with a percentage value and is relative to the width of the browser window. You can also combine fixed- and variable-width settings, as described in the following table.

| Column width | Table width | Resulting column width |
|---|---|---|
| 100 pixels | 500 pixels | 100 pixels |
| 100 pixels | 85% of browser | 100 pixels |
| 10% (of table) | 500 pixels | 50 pixels (10% of 500 pixels) |
| 10% (of table) | 85% (of browser) | 8.5% of browser (10% of 85%) |

*Do it!*

### C-1:   Working with fixed and variable widths

| Here's how | Here's why |
|---|---|
| 1  Preview products.html in your browser | You'll change some of the columns from fixed widths to variable widths. |
| Point to the right edge of the browser window, as shown | 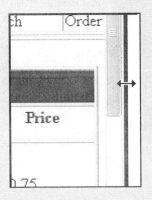 |
| | The pointer changes to a double-sided arrow to enable resizing. |
| Drag the right edge of the window back and forth | To resize the window. Notice that the tables remain the same size, because they have fixed widths, so their size isn't calculated relative to the size of the browser window. |
| Close the browser | |

2  In the Products table, click within the cell containing "Product"

   In the W box, enter **100**    (In the Property inspector.) To set the width of the first column to 100 pixels.

3  In the tag selector, click the **<table>** tag

To select the entire table. You'll change the width of the table from a fixed width to a percentage of the browser window. The options in the Property inspector change with the selection.

   In the W box, enter **85**

   In the list next to the W box, select **%**

| W | 85 | % | ∨ |
| H | | pixels | ∨ |

To make the table width 85% of the width of the browser window.

4  In the Navigation Bar table, click the cell containing "Home"    You'll apply a variable width to cells (columns) in this row.

   Select the row    Drag to the far-right cell in the row.

   In the Property inspector, in the W box, enter **12%**    To give the cells in this row a width of 12% of the table's width.

5  In the Products table, select the Price column    You'll align the price data in this column.

   In the Property inspector, click ▤    (The Align Right button.) To align the data in these cells to the right.

6  Center the spice images in their cells    Select the column and click Align Center in the Property inspector.

7  Save the page and preview it in Internet Explorer

   Resize the browser window    Drag the edge of the window back and forth. The Products table expands and contracts as the window changes size. However, the right and left columns remain the same size, because they still have fixed widths.

   Close the browser

## Borders and cell padding

When you create a table, the borders are displayed by default. Because of this, it's easier for you to see the columns and rows while you're building the table and working with the table content.

Default settings also apply to the spacing inside cells, to horizontal and vertical alignment, and to other formatting options. Depending on the purpose of your table, you might not want to display the table borders, or you might want to change the spacing between cells or change the spacing between cell content and cell borders. If you create a table for layout purposes, you probably want to disable the table borders, so that the table's framework isn't visible.

Exhibit 4-7 shows two versions of the same table. The first uses the default settings for cell borders and cell spacing. In the second table, the borders are disabled, and the spacing inside the cells is increased. This spacing between a cell's borders and its content, is called *cell padding*. You can change the amount of cell padding in the Cell Pad box in the Property inspector.

| Featured Products | | |
|---|---|---|
| Product | Description | Price |
| | Cinnamon is one of the most popular of our spices, due to its sweet flavor and prominent role in baked goods and candies. Cinnamon is also wonderful in stews and sauces. | $10.75 |
| | Nutmeg comes from the seed of a tropical tree. It has a sweet, rich and aromatic flavor that complements meats, vegetables, tomato sauces, and baked goods. | $3.95 |
| | Bay leaf is a versatile herb that goes extremely well with soups, stews, roasts, and anything that is simmered or cooked slowly. | $5.75 |

| Featured Products | | |
|---|---|---|
| Product | Description | Price |
| | Cinnamon is one of the most popular of our spices, due to its sweet flavor and prominent role in baked goods and candies. Cinnamon is also wonderful in stews and sauces. | $10.75 |
| | Nutmeg comes from the seed of a tropical tree. It has a sweet, rich and aromatic flavor that complements meats, vegetables, tomato sauces, and baked goods. | $3.95 |
| | Bay leaf is a versatile herb that goes extremely well with soups, stews, roasts, and anything that is simmered or cooked slowly. | $5.75 |

*Exhibit 4-7: Two tables with different settings for borders and cell padding*

*Do it!*          **C-2:    Customizing cell properties**

| Here's how | Here's why |
|---|---|
| 1  Select the Products table | You'll adjust the cell padding and borders. |
| 2  In the Property inspector, in the CellPad box, enter **10** | To increase the cell padding to 10 pixels. |
| 3  Edit the Border box to read **0** | To disable the table borders. |
| 4  At the top of the page, select the outer Navigation Bar table and disable its borders | |
| 5  Save the page and preview it in Internet Explorer | Only the borders for the nested Navigation Bar table are visible. |
|    Close the browser | |
|    Close products.html | |

# Topic D:  Layout tables

This topic covers the following Adobe ACE exam objective for Dreamweaver CS3.

| # | Objective |
|---|-----------|
| **3.8** | Given a method, lay out a page. (Methods include: Table Layout, Layers, Expanded Tables mode.) |

*Explanation*

In Dreamweaver's Table Layout mode, you can use tables to create page layouts quickly. You can also place multiple layout tables on a page. By doing this, you can customize the table grid and properties of one layout section without affecting other sections.

## Creating layout tables

To create a layout table:

1   On the Insert bar, activate the Layout tab.

2   Choose View, Table Mode, Layout mode.

3   On the Insert bar, click the Draw Layout Table button.

4   Point to an empty area of the document. When the pointer changes to a crosshair, click the page.

5   Using the Property inspector, resize and format the layout table as needed.

### D-1: Creating a layout table

| Here's how | Here's why |
|---|---|
| 1 Open aboutus.html | You'll create a layout for this page by using layout tables. |
| 2 On the insert bar, activate the Layout tab | To display the Layout items. |
| Choose **View**, **Table Mode**, **Layout mode** | To switch to Layout mode. The Getting Started in Layout Mode dialog box appears. |
| Click **OK** | |
| 3 In the document toolbar, click | To expand the Visual Aid list. |
| From the list, select **Hide All Visual Aids** | To hide the visual aids for the layout tables. |
| 4 Click | (The Draw Layout Table button on the Insert bar.) To start a layout table. |
| Point to the blank area below the Home button, as shown | HOME \| AB  +  The pointer changes to a crosshair. |
| Click the page | To place a blank layout table at this position. |
| 5 In the Property inspector, in the Width box, enter **750** | To apply a fixed width of 750 pixels. |
| In the Height box, enter **1638** | To apply a height of 1638 pixels. |
| 6 Save the page | |

### Working with layout cells

*Explanation*

You can resize layout cells and drag them to specific positions within a table. Doing so allows text, images, and other objects inserted in those cells to be positioned precisely where you need them on a Web page. This process is typically easier than creating a complicated series of nested tables. Exhibit 4-8 shows an example of a layout table and individual layout cells.

To insert a layout cell:

1 On the Insert bar, activate the Layout tab.
2 Select Layout mode, if necessary.
3 On the Insert bar, click the Draw Layout Cell button. You can also choose Insert, Layout Objects, Layout Cell.
4 Drag on the page to create a layout cell.
5 Drag the cell to position it exactly where you need it.
6 Resize and format the cell as needed by using the Property inspector.

If you drag within a layout table, Dreamweaver inserts the cell in that table. If you drag on a blank area of the page, Dreamweaver automatically creates a new layout table to hold the cell.

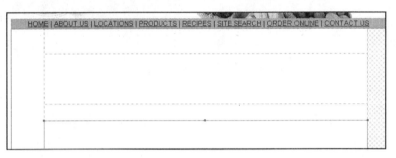

*Exhibit 4-8: A layout table and individual layout cells*

*Do it!*

## D-2: Working with layout cells

| Here's how | Here's why |
|---|---|
| 1 Click ▥ | (The Draw Layout Cell button on the Insert bar.) You'll add layout cells to the layout table to act as containers and to provide spacing. |
| Drag inside the layout table, as shown | HOME \| ABOUT US \| LOCAT |
| | To create a layout cell within the existing layout table. |
| Click an edge of the layout cell | To select it. |

2  Drag the layout cell past the border of the layout table

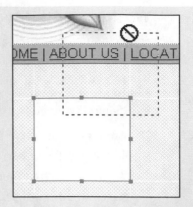

The pointer changes to indicate that you can't drag to this location.

Release the mouse button

The layout cell snaps back to its original position. You can't move the layout cell to a position where it overlaps or collides with another table object.

3  Drag the layout cell to the top-left corner of the layout table

Click the border of the layout cell

(If necessary.) To select it.

4  Set the Width to **65** and the Height to **1638**

In the Property inspector.

5  Draw another layout cell and position it next to the first, as shown

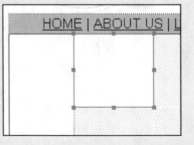

Click the Draw Layout Cell button on the Insert bar. Then drag in the layout table and drag the new layout cell to the corner.

Set the Width to **648** and the Height to **50**

6 Insert a new layout cell at the corner where the first two layout cells meet, as shown

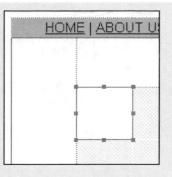

Set the Width to **648** and the Height to **100**

7 Add another layout cell with a Width of **648** and a Height of **33**

8 Add another layout cell with a Width of **648** and a Height of **840**

The table should look like the one shown in Exhibit 4-8.

9 Save the page

## Adding content to layout cells

*Explanation*    You can add text, images, and other page elements to a layout cell. To add text, an image, or another asset from a file to a cell:

1 Drag the file from the Files panel to the layout cell.
2 Resize and reposition the layout cell, as needed.

*Do it!*    **D-3:    Adding content to a layout table**

| Here's how | Here's why |
|---|---|
| 1 In the Files pane, navigate to the images folder | (In the current unit folder.) You'll add text and images to the layout table you created. |
| 2 Drag **aboutus.jpg** to the second layout cell from the top | The Image Tag Accessibility Attributes dialog box appears. |
| In the Alternate Text box, type **About us** | |
| Click **OK** | |

The image displays in the layout cell.

3  Drag **heading-allspicedup.gif** to the next layout cell

(The cell under the existing image.) The Image Tag Accessibility Attributes dialog box appears.

In the Alternate Text box, type **All Spiced Up**

Click **OK**

4  Click the border of the layout cell

To select it.

In the Property inspector, in the Vert list, select **Bottom**

To align the image with the bottom of the layout cell.

Collapse the images folder

Click the plus sign.

5  Drag **aboutus.txt** to the next layout cell

To insert text into the page. The Insert Document dialog box opens.

Click **Insert the Contents**

If necessary.

Click **Text only** and click **OK**

To insert the text from the file and close the dialog box.

On the Insert bar, click **Standard**

To switch to Standard mode.

6  Save the page and preview it in Internet Explorer

Close the browser

7  Close all open files

# Unit summary: Tables

*Topic A*       In this topic, you learned about **tables**. You learned how to insert a table, create a **header row**, insert text and images, and create **nested tables**.

*Topic B*       In this topic, you learned how to select and format **cells**, **rows**, and **columns**. You also learned how to **merge cells** and insert rows and columns.

*Topic C*       In this topic, you learned how to fine-tune **table properties**, including column and table **widths**, **cell borders**, and **cell padding**.

*Topic D*       In this topic, you learned how to create a **layout table** and add layout cells. You learned how to arrange cells, change their dimensions, and insert content.

## Independent practice activity

In this activity, you'll create a nested table and add images and text to it, add rows to an existing table, and place a layout table and layout cells on a page.

1  Choose **Site**, **New Site** to start the Site Definition Wizard.

2  Enter **Outlander Tables Practice** as the site name.

3  Enter **http://www.outlanderspices.com** for the site URL.

4  Click **Next** and then click **Next** again.

5  On the Editing Files, Part 3 page, navigate to the Practice folder in the current unit folder.

6  On the Sharing files page, choose **None** as the server connection, and click **Next**.

7  Click **Done** to complete the wizard.

8  Open locations.html.

9  Below the sub navigation bar, create a table that consists of three rows, one column, and a width of **80%**. (*Hint:* Click below the sub navigation bar to place the insertion point, then click the Table button in the Insert bar.)

10  Center the table beneath the navigation bars. Make sure the table border is disabled.

11  In the top row, insert the image usa-map.gif and center it. The image is located in the images subfolder.

12  In the bottom row, insert a nested table that consists of four rows and two columns. Make the nested table **475** pixels wide, and center it. (*Hint:* Click to place the insertion point in the bottom row before you click the Table button in the Insert bar.)

13  Set the left column of the nested table to **175** pixels wide and the right column to **300** pixels wide.

14  Add the text shown in Exhibit 4-9. (*Hint:* Use the Property inspector to format the text and the cells.)

15  Above Nevada, add a row for Oregon with the following locations:
    - Shopper's Paradise, Portland
    - Port Plaza, Santa Barbara

16  Open sitemap.html. As shown in Exhibit 4-10, create a layout table with layout cells, and insert **search.jpg**.

17 Save and close all open files.

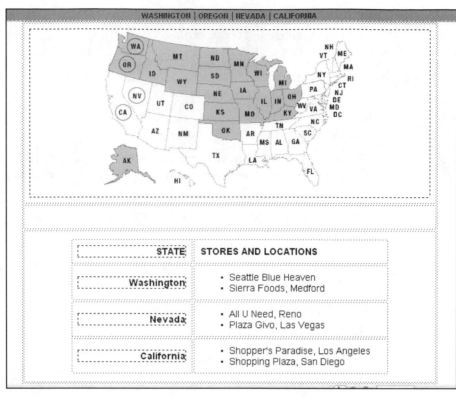

*Exhibit 4-9: The locations page after completing step 14*

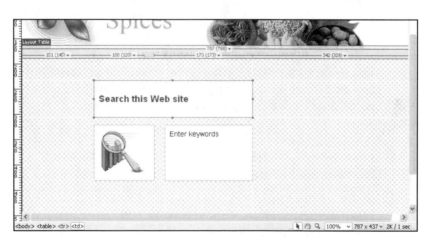

*Exhibit 4-10: The sitemap page after completing step 16*

## Review questions

1  A nested table is:

   A  A table that's inserted into a row of another table

   B  A table that's inserted into a cell of another table

   C  A table with fixed dimensions

   D  A table with flexible dimensions

2  How can you create a new layout table? [Choose all that apply.]

   A  Switch to the Layout menu, then select Layout mode. On the Insert bar, click the Layout Table button, then click the page where you want the table.

   B  Create a basic HTML table. Double-click the table, then select Convert To Layout Table, and click OK.

   C  Choose Insert, Table. In the dialog box, select Layout Table, then click OK.

   D  Switch to the Layout menu, then select Layout mode. On the Insert bar, click the Draw Layout Cell button, then drag on the page.

3  How can you add a layout cell to a layout table? [Choose all that apply.]

   A  Right-click in the layout table and choose Insert, Layout Cell, then drag in the table to create the cell.

   B  Choose Insert, Layout Object, Layout Cell, then drag in the table to create the cell.

   C  On the Insert bar, click the Draw Layout Cell button, then drag in the table to create the cell.

   D  On the Insert bar, click the Draw Layout Table button, then drag in the table to create the cell.

4  The number of columns in a table is determined by:

   A  The number of rows

   B  The number of column tags

   C  The number of cells in each row

   D  The value of the column attributes

5  The width of a column is determined by:

   A  The width you set for the first cell in the column

   B  The width you set for the table

   C  The width you set for an intersecting row

   D  The width of the largest cell in that column

6 A table has a fixed width of 600 pixels. A cell inside this table has a width of 20%, and no other width is specified for another cell in its column. How many pixels wide is this column?

A 80 pixels

B 60 pixels

C 160 pixels

D 180 pixels

E 120 pixels

7 Cell padding is:

A The space between a cell's borders and content

B The space between cells

C The space between rows and columns

D The space between a table and the bottom of the page

8 How can you view tables in Expanded Tables Mode? [Choose all that apply.]

A Select View, Table Mode, Expanded Tables Mode.

B Double-click a table border.

C Ctrl-click a table border.

D In the Insert bar, in the Layout category, click the Expanded Tables Mode button.

# Unit 5

## Images

**Unit time: 25 minutes**

Complete this unit, and you'll know how to:

**A** Choose appropriate image formats, insert images, and modify image properties.

**B** Insert and modify background images and write effective alternate text.

# Topic A: Image formats and tags

This topic covers the following Adobe ACE exam objective for Dreamweaver CS3.

| # | Objective |
|---|-----------|
| 2.7 | List and describe the features Dreamweaver provides for Accessibility Standards/Section 508 compliance. |

## Images on the Web

*Explanation*

Images are an integral part of Web design. They catch the user's eye, they can introduce a unique artistic aspect to site designs, and they can often deliver information in a way that text can't. For example, images of products give potential buyers visual information that can't be matched by a text description.

File size is a vital consideration when using images on Web pages. Large image files can take a long time to load in a user's browser. Try to keep your image file sizes as small as possible without sacrificing quality.

You can find images for your Web site from a variety of sources, including the following:

- Some Web sites offer free images for downloading. Make sure that you read the site's downloading policy before you use any free images. Unauthorized use of images usually qualifies as copyright infringement.

- You can purchase image collections on CD-ROM or directly from Web sites.

- You can create your own images. For example, you can take digital photos and then use a program, such as Adobe Photoshop, to modify and optimize your images for the Web. You can also create images that aren't based on a photograph. Adobe Photoshop and Illustrator are two popular programs that enable you to create your own Web graphics.

### File formats

The three main image formats currently supported by browsers are GIF, JPEG, and PNG. GIF images, which can contain a maximum of 256 colors, are best used for images with relatively few colors and with areas of flat color, such as line drawings, logos, and illustrations. GIFs also support animation and transparency. The GIF format isn't recommended for photographs or illustrations with complex color gradations. When you save simple images of fewer than 256 colors, GIF uses a *lossless* compression algorithm, which means that no image data are discarded to compress the image.

The JPEG format supports more than 16 million colors, so it's best for photographs and images that have many subtle color shadings. JPEG uses *lossy* compression, which means that some image data is discarded when the file is saved. You can select the degree of compression applied when saving the file, with the following tradeoff: the smaller the file, the lower the image quality.

The PNG format combines some of the best features of JPEG and GIF. It supports more than 16 million colors, so it's ideal for photos and complex drawings. It can use a variety of lossless compression algorithms, and it supports many levels of transparency, allowing areas of an image to appear transparent or semitransparent. The downside of

PNG is that some browsers don't support it. The following table summarizes these three image file formats.

|  | **GIF** | **JPEG** | **PNG** |
|---|---|---|---|
| **Best used for:** | Simple images with few colors | Photographs | Photographs or simple images |
| **Maximum colors** | 256 | More than 16 million | More than 16 million |
| **Compression** | Lossless | Lossy | Lossless |
| **Transparency** | One level (complete transparency) | Not supported | Multiple levels |
| **Browser support** | All | All | Netscape 6 and later, Internet Explorer 7 and later, Firefox, Safari |

*Do it!*

## A-1:   Discussing image formats

| Questions | Answers |
|---|---|
| 1  Which image formats are best for photographs? |  |
| 2  Which image formats support transparency? |  |
| 3  Why should you be careful when using the PNG format? |  |
| 4  True or false: The GIF format and JPEG format support the same number of colors |  |
| 5  A corporate logo that contains text and six colors is probably best saved in what image format? |  |

### Image-based text

*Explanation*

You can add text to a page in the form of an image. If you have a graphics application, such as Adobe Photoshop, Adobe Illustrator, or Adobe Fireworks, you can create text in a graphic file and save it with the appropriate file extension (typically .gif). Image-based text is often used for logos or for headings that require special styling that can't be provided by HTML or CSS.

#### Advantages

By using image-based text, you can also use exotic fonts that your users aren't likely to have on their machines and would, therefore, be otherwise unable to display. You might also want to apply special effects, such as drop shadows or embossing, which you can't create by using actual text.

#### Disadvantages

Image-based text also has its disadvantages. Images increase a page's overall size and download time. Using too many of these images can make a page exceedingly slow for some users. Also, because the images aren't text, the content isn't searchable by search engines, or by the browser's Find function. You can minimize this limitation by always specifying appropriate alternate text for your images. In the case of image-based text, your alternate text should duplicate the text in the image.

*Do it!*

### A-2: Inserting images

| Here's how | Here's why |
|---|---|
| 1 Choose **Site, New Site...** | To open the Site Definition Wizard. You'll create a Web site. |
| 2 For the site name, enter **Outlander - Images** | |
| For the HTTP address, enter **http://www.outlanderspices.com** | |
| Click **Next** | |
| Click **Next** | The Editing Files, Part 3 screen appears. |
| 3 Click 🗀 | To open the "Choose local root folder for Outlander Spices" dialog box. |
| 4 Browse to the current unit folder | |
| Open the Outlander Spices folder and click **Select** | |
| Click **Next** | The Sharing Files screen appears. |
| 5 From the top list, select **None** | |
| Click **Next** | |
| Click **Done** | To create the site. |

| | |
|---|---|
| 6 In the Files panel, expand the Site folder | If necessary. |
| 7 Open recipes.html | (From the Files panel.) You'll replace the title of each recipe with a graphic that has a drop-shadow effect. |
| 8 Delete **Princely Potatoes** | Select the text and press Delete. |
| Open the images folder | |
| 9 Drag **heading-potatoes.gif** to the location of the deleted text | (From the images folder.) The Image Tag Accessibility Attributes dialog box appears. |
| In the Alternate text box, type **Princely Potatoes** | To give this image alternate text that matches the image's content, so that search engines can index the text. |
| Click **OK** | To close the dialog box and insert the image. |
| 10 Verify that the image is placed as shown | |

This image will serve as the new heading for the Princely Potatoes recipe.

| | |
|---|---|
| 11 Delete **Chicken Stuffed with Spices** | |
| Make heading-chicken.gif the new heading | Drag the image above the recipe, on the same line as the Princely Potatoes heading. In the Image Tag Accessibility Attributes dialog box, enter appropriate alternate text, and click OK. |
| 12 Save recipes.html | |

## Image attributes

*Explanation*

When you drag an image onto a page, Dreamweaver writes the HTML code required to embed the image. This code consists of the image tag <img> and several attributes, which are properties for the element. The location of the <img> tag tells the browser where to embed the file, and the src attribute tells the browser where to locate the image file. The attributes of the <img> tag are described in the following table.

| Attribute | Use | Description |
|---|---|---|
| src | Required | Specifies the URL or path to the image file. |
| alt | Recommended | Specifies alternate text. If the browser can't display the image, alternate text allows access to the text in the image, or a description of the image, whichever is more appropriate. |
| height | Recommended | Specifies the height of the image. |
| width | Recommended | Specifies the width of the image. |
| align | Optional | Aligns an image with text on the same line. |
| border | Optional | Specifies the pixel width of the border around an image that acts as a link. |

### Image properties

You can set image properties by using the Property inspector. The options shown in Exhibit 5-1 appear in the Property inspector when you select an image.

*Exhibit 5-1: The Property inspector when an image is selected*

### Alternate text

You should always create alternate text for your images, so that users with alternative devices, such as screen readers or Braille printers, can access the text content of an image or its description or context in the page. You've already entered alternate text when embedding an image for the first time. If you're dealing with an image that's already been added to a page, you can select the image and then enter alternate text in the Alt box in the Property inspector.

In some browsers, including Internet Explorer, alternate text appears as a ScreenTip when you point to the image, as shown in Exhibit 5-2.

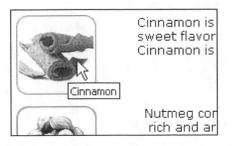

*Exhibit 5-2: Alternate text is displayed as a ScreenTip in some browsers*

*Do it!*

## A-3:    Modifying image properties

| Here's how | Here's why |
|---|---|
| 1  Select the image shown | |
| | You'll specify alternate text for this image. |
| In the Property inspector, click ▽ | (If necessary.) To expand the Property inspector. |
| In the Alt box, enter **Princely Potatoes photo** | There's no text in this image, so it's best to provide a brief description of its contents. |
| 2  Click ▤ | (In the Property inspector.) To align the image to the left of its table cell. |
| 3  Apply alternate text to the other recipe image | Select the image, and then enter an appropriate description in the Alt box in the Property inspector. |
| 4  Align the image to the left | |
| 5  Save the page and preview it in Internet Explorer | |
| Point to any image | A ScreenTip displays the alternate text you specified. |
| Close the browser | |

# Topic B: Background images

*Explanation*

You can use images as background illustrations for an element, such as a table, or for an entire Web page. When you do so, you should always be sure that the background doesn't detract from the readability of your text.

## Applying background images

By default, background images repeat across and downward to occupy an element's entire dimensions. This repetition is called *tiling*. If you're working with a background image for an entire page, the image might tile several times to occupy the space, depending on the size of the image relative to the size of the browser window.

For example, if the image of peppers shown in Exhibit 5-3 is inserted as a background for a table, the image tiles to fill the width and height of the table, as shown in Exhibit 5-4. When selecting a background image, choose one that doesn't detract from the foreground of the page or make the text difficult to read. For example, the descriptions and prices in Exhibit 5-4 are difficult to read against the underlying peppers.

With CSS, you can prevent an image from tiling so that it appears only once on the page, table, or other page element. You can also specify that the image tiles only horizontally or only vertically.

*Exhibit 5-3: An example of a background image*

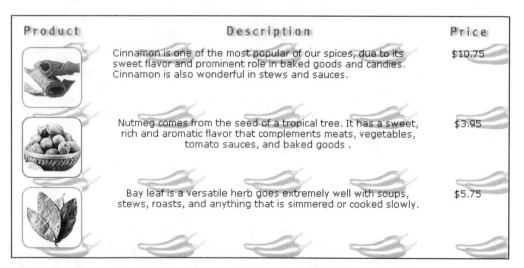

*Exhibit 5-4: A small image used as a table background, tiling in both directions*

To apply a background image to a page:

1 Click anywhere on the page.

2 In the Property inspector, click Page Properties to open the Page Properties dialog box.

3 In the Category list, select Appearance.

4 Click Browse to open the Select Image Source dialog box.

5    Navigate to the desired image file and click OK.

6    Click OK to close the Page Properties dialog box and apply the background image.

To apply a background image to a layout table:

1    Select the layout table.

2    In the Tag Inspector panel group, in the Attributes panel, expand the Browser specific attribute group.

3    Click the value for background.

4    Drag the Point-to-File icon to an image file in the Files panel, or click the Browse button and navigate to an image file.

To apply a background image to an ordinary HTML table:

1    Click in the table.

2    Expand the Property inspector (if necessary).

3    Drag the Point-to-File icon next to the BG Image box to an image file in the Files panel, or click the Browse button and navigate to an image file.

**Tracing images**

If you're working with a design mock-up that was created in a graphics application, such as Adobe Illustrator or Adobe Photoshop, you can use it as a tracing image. The tracing image appears as a page background, and you can use it to arrange page elements as you create the page. Tracing images aren't part of the actual page, so they aren't visible if you preview the page in a browser, or when you upload the final site to a server.

To add a tracing image, open the Page Properties dialog box, then select the Tracing Image category, as shown in Exhibit 5-5. In addition to selecting a graphic to use for the tracing image, you can also use the Transparency slider to control its opacity.

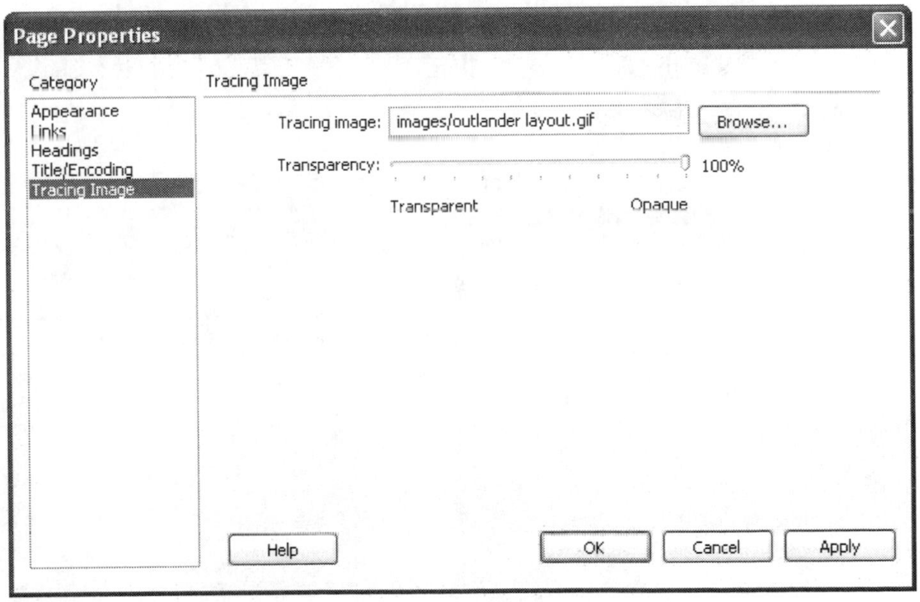

*Exhibit 5-5: Tracing image properties in the Page Properties dialog box*

By default, tracing images are positioned in the upper-left corner of the page. However, you can reposition them on the page by choosing an option from the Tracing Image submenu in the View menu.

*Do it!*

## B-1:   Applying a background image

| Here's how | Here's why |
|---|---|
| 1 In the Files panel, expand the images folder | (If necessary.) You'll apply a background image to a table. |
| 2 In recipes.html, click anywhere in the navigation links table | To place the insertion point. |
| In the Tag selector, click the **<table>** tag | <br>To ensure that you've selected the correct table. |
| 3 In the Property inspector, drag the Point-to-File icon, as shown | (Drag the icon that's next to the Bg Image box to greenbar.gif in the Files panel.) |
| | |
| | To apply greenbar.gif as the background image for the selected table. The image gives the navigation bar a shadow on the bottom. |
| 4 Click on a blank part of the page | To deselect the table. |
| 5 In the document toolbar, click | To expand the Visual Aid list. |
| From the list, select **Hide All Visual Aids** | To see the background image more clearly. |
| 6 Show visual aids again | |
| 7 Save and close recipes.html | |

*FTP. EZBidavctons.com*
*/var/www/Hyml*

# Unit summary: Images

**Topic A**  In this topic, you learned about the **GIF**, **JPEG**, and **PNG** image formats. You learned the advantages and disadvantages of using image-based text, and you learned how to **insert an image** in a page. Then you learned about the attributes of the image tag, and you learned the importance of writing effective **alternate text** for your images.

**Topic B**  In this topic, you learned how to apply an image as a **background**. You also learned about background image **tiling** and using a **tracing image** to reproduce a design mock-up.

*Students*
*Fd @ 5Jy 29*

## Independent practice activity

In this activity, you'll replace text with images and add backgrounds to tables.

1  Choose **Site**, **New Site** to start the Site Definition Wizard.

2  Enter **Outlander Images Practice** as the site name.

3  Enter **http://www.outlanderspices.com** for the site URL.

4  Click **Next** twice.

5  On the Editing Files, Part 3 page, navigate to the Practice folder in the current unit folder.

6  On the Sharing files page, choose **None** as the server connection, and click **Next**.

7  Click **Done** to complete the wizard.

8  Open aboutus.html.

9  Replace the text, "All Spiced Up," with heading-allspicedup.gif. Specify appropriate alternate text for the image.

10  Replace the text, "Expansion project," with heading-expansion.gif. Specify appropriate alternate text.

11  Apply greenbar.gif as the background for the navigation row in the top table, as shown in Exhibit 5-6.

12  Save and close aboutus.html.

*Exhibit 5-6: The topbar.gif background after step 11*

## Review questions

1 Which of the following are advantages of using image-based text? [Choose all that apply.]

   A Image-based text allows you to use exotic fonts and text effects.

   B Image-based text loads faster than normal text.

   C Image-based text can be more eye-catching than normal text.

   D Image-based text is easier to read than normal text.

2 Which of the following are disadvantages of using image-based text? [Choose all that apply.]

   A Too many of them increase a page's overall size and download time.

   B The content in the image can't be indexed by search engines.

   C The alternate text you specify for them can't be indexed by search engines.

   D Text in images is usually harder to read than actual text.

3 When your image contains text, your alternate text should:

   A Describe the content of the image.

   B Duplicate the text that appears in the image.

   C Be omitted.

   D Provide more information about the text.

4 Alternate text for a photograph without text should:

   A Briefly describe the content of the image.

   B Indicate that the image doesn't contain text.

   C Be omitted.

   D Indicate that it's a photographic image.

5 How can you add a tracing image to a page?

   A Press and hold Ctrl, then drag an image to the page.

   B Open the Page Properties dialog box and select the Tracing Image category, then select the image you want to use and set options for it.

   C Choose Insert, Image. In the dialog box, select the image you want to use, check Tracing Image, and click OK.

   D Add the image to the page, then right-click the image and choose Convert To Tracing Image.

6  When you insert a background image, by default the image:

A  Tiles horizontally.

B  Tiles vertically.

C  Tiles horizontally and vertically.

D  Tiles diagonally.

# Unit 6

## Links

**Unit time: 45 minutes**

Complete this unit, and you'll know how to:

**A** Create links to other pages and resources, create named anchors and link to them, and create e-mail links.

**B** Create an image map.

**C** Apply CSS styles to link states.

# Topic A:  Creating links

*Explanation*

Links provide the functionality that makes the Web the interconnected world that it is. Links enable users to navigate to other pages in a site, to external pages and resources, and to specific sections of a page.

### Link destinations and types

When a user clicks a link, the browser navigates to the destination specified in the link. You can set a link to open in the current browser window or in a new one. These destination types are called link *targets*.

- A *Self* target opens the link destination in the current window.
- A *Blank* target opens the link destination in a new window.

### Link types

There are three basic link types:

- *Local* links navigate to other pages and resources in a Web site.
- *External* links navigate to pages and resources outside a Web site.
- *Named-anchor* links navigate to specific sections of a Web page. Named-anchor links are also called *bookmark links* or *intra-document links*.

### Local links

Local links are links to pages and resources within a Web site, so specifying the path is relatively simple. If the destination file resides in the same directory as the page that contains the link, you can simply type the file name in the Link box in the Property inspector. If the link destination resides in a different folder, you need to specify the folder, followed by the file name.

To create a local link:

1 Select the text or image that you want to serve as the link.
2 In the Property inspector, do one of the following:
   - Next to the Link box, drag the Point-to-File icon to the destination file in the Files panel.
   - Click the Browse button and navigate to the destination file.

*Do it!*

### A-1:  Creating a link to a page in your site

| Here's how | Here's why |
|---|---|
| 1 Choose **Site, New Site...** | To open the Site Definition Wizard. You'll create a Web site. |
| 2 For the site name, enter **Outlander - Links** | |
| For the HTTP address, enter **http://www.outlanderspices.com** | |
| Click **Next** | |
| Click **Next** | The Editing Files, Part 3 screen appears. |

| | |
|---|---|
| 3  Click 🗀 | To open the "Choose local root folder for Outlander Spices" dialog box. |
| 4  Browse to the current unit folder | |
| Open the Outlander Spices folder and click **Select** | |
| Click **Next** | The Sharing Files screen appears. |
| 5  From the top list, select **None** | |
| Click **Next** | |
| Click **Done** | To create the site. |
| 6  In the Files panel, expand the Site folder | If necessary. |
| 7  Open aboutus.html | From the Files panel. |
| 8  In the topmost navigation bar, double-click **Home** | To select it. You'll create a link that navigates to the Home page. |
| 9  In the Property inspector, click the folder icon, as shown | |
| | To specify the path of the link target. The Select File dialog box appears. |
| 10  Select **index.html** | (In the Outlander Spices folder, in the current unit folder.) To specify the link target. |
| Click **OK** | The word "Home" is now a link. By default, a link appears as blue, underlined text to distinguish it from normal text. |
| 11  Save aboutus.html | |
| 12  Preview the page in your browser | (Press F12) To see the link in action. |
| Click **Home** | The browser navigates to index.html. |
| Close the browser | |

## Named anchors

*Explanation*

Named anchors can mark an element on a Web page as a target, so that any link navigates directly to that position on the page. This feature is useful, for long pages, as an alternative to scrolling. You can also link to a named anchor on another page in your site.

To create a named anchor:

1 Choose View, Visual Aids, Invisible Elements (if necessary), so that named-anchor tags appear in the document window.
2 Place the insertion point at the target location.
3 On the Insert bar, select Common and then click the Named Anchor button. The Named Anchor dialog box appears.
4 In the Anchor Name box, type a name for the anchor.
5 Click OK.

To link to a named anchor, select the text or image that will serve as the link. Then, in the Property inspector, do one of the following:

- In the Link box, type # (the number sign), followed immediately by the name of the anchor: `#anchorName`.
- Drag the Point-to-File icon beside the Link box to the named anchor.

*Do it!*    **A-2:    Creating and linking to a named anchor**

| Here's how | Here's why |
|---|---|
| 1 In the document toolbar, click [eye icon] | To expand the Visual Aid list. |
| From the list, select **Invisible Elements** | (If necessary.) To display invisible elements, including symbols for named anchors. You'll insert a named anchor and create a link to it. |
| 2 Place the insertion point to the right of the large logo image | |
| On the Insert bar, activate the Common tab | (If necessary.) To display the common insert items. |
| 3 Click [anchor icon] | (The Named Anchor button.) The Named Anchor dialog box appears. |
| In the Anchor Name box, enter **top** | |
| Click **OK** | |
| | The anchor symbol appears. |
| 4 Scroll to the bottom of the page, then select the text **Go to top** | You'll make this text a link to the *top* anchor. |
| In the Property inspector, in the Link box, type **#top** | |
| 5 Save aboutus.html | |
| 6 Preview the page in your browser | To see the link in action. |
| Scroll to the bottom of the page and click **Go to Top** | The browser navigates to the named anchor at the top of the page. |
| Close the browser | |
| 7 How might you use named anchors in your own Web site? | |

## External links

*Explanation*

External links navigate to a page or resource on another Web site. You can also create a link that launches the user's default e-mail program, begins an outgoing message, and inserts the e-mail address of your choice in the To field.

To create an external link:

1  Select the text or image that you want to serve as the link.
2  In the Property inspector, in the Link box, type the complete URL of the destination page or resource.

To create an e-mail link:

1  Select the text or image that you want to serve as the link.
2  In the Property inspector, in the Link box, type **mailto:** followed by the e-mail address to which you want the message to be sent.

If no e-mail application is configured on the user's computer when an e-mail link is clicked, a dialog box appears, prompting the user to configure an e-mail application.

*Do it!*

## A-3:    Creating external links and e-mail links

| Here's how | Here's why |
|---|---|
| 1  Open index.html | (From the Files panel.) You'll create an external link and an e-mail link. |
| 2  Select the ISO 9000 award image |  |
| | (Near the bottom of the page.) You'll make this image an external link. |
| 3  In the Link box, type **http://www.iso.org** | In the Property inspector. |
| Press ↵ ENTER | The image is now a link to the specified URL. |
| 4  In the navigation bar, select **Contact Us** | You'll make this text an e-mail link. |
| In the Link box, type **mailto:info@outlanderspices.com** | |
| Press ↵ ENTER | When the user clicks the link, his or her default e-mail program opens, with this address used for the outgoing message. |
| 5  Save index.html | |
| Preview the page in your browser | |
| 6  Click **Contact Us** | An e-mail message with the specified address opens in the default e-mail application. (If no e-mail application is configured on the computer, you're prompted to configure an e-mail application.) |
| Close the e-mail message | If applicable. |
| 7  Click the ISO 9000 award image | To view the ISO Web site. |
| Close the browser | |
| 8  Close index.html | |

# Topic B:  Image maps

*Explanation*

An *image map* is an image that contains multiple links. Various areas within the image, called *hotspots*, are linked to various targets. Image maps provide a unique, interactive design tool that you can use in a variety of contexts.

## Creating an image map

A hotspot in an image map can be any size and can be any of several shapes: oval, circle, rectangle, square, or irregularly shaped polygon.

To create an image map:

1   Select the image in the document window.
2   Expand the Property inspector (if necessary).
3   In the Map Name box, enter a unique name for the image map.
4   Click the Rectangular Hotspot Tool, the Oval Hotspot Tool, or the Polygon Hotspot Tool.
5   Drag to draw the outline, or, if you're using the Polygon tool, click the corners of the shape to begin the outline.
6   Use the Point-to-File icon or the Browse button next to the Link box to link to a local link, a named anchor, or an external link.

*Do it!*

## B-1:   Creating an image map

| **Here's how** | **Here's why** |
|---|---|
| 1  Open locations.html | From the Files panel. |
| Click the image of the U.S. | To select it. |
| In the Property inspector, click ▽ | (If necessary.) To expand the Property inspector. |
| 2  Click ⬚ | The Rectangular Hotspot Tool is in the Property inspector. |
| 3  Point to **OR**, as shown | |
| | (The pointer changes to a crosshair.) You'll insert a hotspot here, so that, when a user clicks the image of Oregon, the browser jumps to the specified destination. |
| Drag over and down to draw a rectangle, as shown | |
| | This defines the clickable region for this link. The Adobe Dreamweaver CS3 dialog box appears. |
| Click **OK** | To acknowledge the prompt and close the dialog box. |
| 4  Observe the Link box | (In the Property inspector.) The # sign is entered automatically because a hotspot link must begin with a number sign. |
| 5  Edit the Link box to read **#Oregon** | Link  #Oregon |
| | To name the anchor to which this hotspot links. |
| Press (↵ ENTER) | To create a link from the rectangular hotspot to this named anchor. |
| 6  In the Alt box, enter **Oregon** | |
| Press (↵ ENTER) | To create alternate text for this hotspot. In some browsers, this appears as a ScreenTip when a user points to the hotspot. |

7 Is the Rectangular Hotspot Tool the most appropriate tool for this hotspot?

Why or why not?

8 Click  (The Polygon Hotspot Tool is in the Property inspector.) You'll create a polygon hotspot.

9 Point to **NV**, as shown

The pointer changes to a crosshair.

Click the top-right corner of the state border, as shown

To set the first point of the hotspot polygon. The Adobe Dreamweaver CS3 dialog box appears.

Click **OK**

To acknowledge the prompt and close the dialog box.

Click the top-left corner of the state border, as shown

To define the second point of the polygon. A line appears between the two points.

10 Continue clicking each corner until the hotspot takes the shape of the state, as shown

11 Create a link to the anchor named **#Nevada**

In the Link box, immediately after the number sign, enter Nevada.

12 Create appropriate alternate text for this hotspot

Enter Nevada in the Alt box.

13 Save locations.html

| 14 | Preview the page in your browser | |
|----|----------------------------------|---|
| 15 | Point to **OR** | A ScreenTip with the alternate text appears. |
| | Click **OR** | To navigate to the named anchor. The page shows the Oregon information. |
| | Scroll up | (If necessary.) To display the map again. |
| | Click **NV** | To navigate to the named anchor. |
| 16 | Close the browser | |
| 17 | Close locations.html | |

# Topic C: Link styles

This topic covers the following Adobe ACE exam objective for Dreamweaver CS3.

| # | Objective |
|---|-----------|
| 3.4 | Create and maintain Cascading Style Sheets (CSS.) |

*Explanation*

By default, text links appear as blue, underlined text. These default styles might suit your Web site design, but blue links might not fit the color scheme of your site. You can use CSS *pseudo-classes* to customize the appearance of links to fit your site's color scheme better. You can also assign styles that act as visual cues to the state of a link.

## Link states

*Link states* define the current condition of a link. There are four link states, as described in the following table.

| State | Description |
|-------|-------------|
| Link | The default state of a link that hasn't been activated in any way. |
| Visited | The state of a link after you click it and its destination page has loaded. In many browsers, visited links appear as purple, underlined text by default. |
| Hover | The state of a link when you point to it. Most browsers don't apply any default formatting to the hover state. |
| Active | The state of a link when you click it but haven't yet released the mouse button. A link is in this state for only a moment. Most browsers don't apply any default formatting to the active state. |

### Visited links

The browser's cache keeps track of links whose destinations have already been viewed. When a link has been visited, the link remains in that state until the browser's cache is cleared. For example, in Internet Explorer, choose Tools, Internet Options, Clear History to reset the browser's list of visited links.

If you recently viewed the page that a link references, it appears in the visited state, even if you didn't click the link.

*Do it!*    ## C-1: Applying link styles

| Here's how | Here's why |
|---|---|
| 1 Switch to aboutus.html | You'll set link styles for each state. |
| 2 In the navigation bar, observe the Home link | 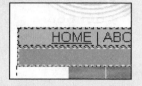 |
| | The link is blue and underlined. This is the default formatting that most browsers apply to links. |
| 3 Expand the CSS panel | If necessary. |
| 4 Click ▣ | To open the New CSS Rule dialog box. |
| 5 Next to Selector Type, select **Advanced** | |
| In the Selector list, select **a:link** | |
| Next to Define in, verify that globalstyles.css is selected | |
| Click **OK** | To create a style for this state and close the dialog box. The CSS Rule Definition dialog box appears. |
| 6 In the Category list, verify that Type is selected | |
| Click the Color box and select the dark blue color **#000066** | ![Color picker showing #000066]  Color:    #000066 |
| Under Decoration, check **none** | To remove the underline. |
| Click **OK** | To format this link state and close the dialog box. The Home link shows the formatting you specified. |

| | |
|---|---|
| 7 Create a CSS rule for **a:visited** | Click the New CSS Rule button in the CSS panel. Then, in the New CSS Rule dialog box, select a:visited from the Selector list, and click OK. |
| Select the dark gray color **#666666** | 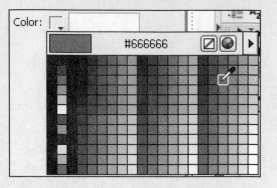 |
| | Click the Color box and select the #666666 swatch. |
| Under Decoration, check **none** | To remove the default underline for the visited state. |
| Click **OK** | |
| 8 Create a CSS rule for **a:hover** | |
| Remove the underline, and give the link state the dark red color **#990000** | |
| 9 Create a CSS rule for **a:active** | |
| Remove the underline, and give the link state the dark red color **#990000** | To make the active style the same as the hover style. |
| 10 Observe the CSS panel | **▼ CSS** ≡ |

The following appears in the CSS panel image:

**▼ CSS**

CSS Styles | AP Elements

| All | Current |

**Summary for Selection**

| | |
|---|---|
| font-family | Arial, Helvetica, san... |
| color (link) | #000066 |
| text-decoration (l... | none |
| color (visited) | #666666 |
| text-decoration (... | none |
| color (hover) | #990000 |
| text-decoration (... | none |
| color (active) | #990000 |

The CSS styles that you created for the link states appear.

11   Activate globalstyles.css

Observe the styles for the four link states

Save and close globalstyles.css

12   Preview aboutus.html in your browser

Observe the Home link                    (In the navigation bar at the top of the page.) The text appears in the gray color that you specified for visited links.

13   Point to **Home**                     The text changes to the dark red color you defined for links in the hover state.

14   Click and hold **Home**               The active state's formatting is the same as that of the hover state.

Release the mouse button                  The browser navigates to the home page, index.html.

Click  ⊙ Back ▾                          (In your browser.) To return to aboutus.html.

15   Click a blank area of the page        To deselect the link. The text changes to the gray color you defined for visited links.

16   Close the browser

Close aboutus.html

# Unit summary: Links

**Topic A**     In this topic, you learned about **links**. You learned about the various link types and targets, and you learned how to create links to pages within a Web site. Then you created **named anchors** and linked to them. Finally, you learned how to create **external links** and **e-mail links**.

**Topic B**     In this topic, you learned how to create an **image map**. You learned how to draw **hotspots** on an image map with various shape tools and to link those hotspots to other destinations.

**Topic C**     In this topic, you learned about **link states**. You learned that applying styles to link states allows you to fit your links into your color scheme and gives users feedback about the links on a page. You learned how to apply CSS styles to each state: link, visited, hover, and active.

## Independent practice activity

In this activity, you'll create named anchors and link to them, and then you'll create external links, an e-mail link, and an image map. You'll also apply link styles.

1  Choose **Site**, **New Site** to start the Site Definition Wizard.

2  Enter **Outlander Links Practice** as the site name.

3  Enter **http://www.outlanderspices.com** for the site URL.

4  Click **Next** twice.

5  On the Editing Files, Part 3 page, navigate to the Practice folder in the current unit folder.

6  On the Sharing files page, choose **None**, as the server connection, and click **Next**.

7  Click **Done** to complete the wizard.

8  Open aboutus.html from the Files panel.

9  Drag a named anchor to the right of the text graphic, All Spiced Up, and name it **SpicedUp**.

10  At the top of the table, link the matching text ("All Spiced Up") to this anchor.

11  Create a named anchor for the "Expansion Project" graphic and name it **Expansion**. Link its matching text to this named anchor.

12  Create a named anchor for the "The Project Team" graphic and name it **Team**. Link its matching text to this named anchor. Save aboutus.html, preview the page in your browser, and test the three links.

13  Close the browser and close aboutus.html.

14  Open index.html.

15  For the About Us, Locations, Products, and Recipes items in the navigation bar, create links to their corresponding Web pages. For Contact Us, specify a link to the e-mail address **contact@outlanderspices.com**. (The page files are in the Outlander Spices folder in the current unit folder.)

16  Apply color styles of your choice to the three links, using the **a:link**, **a:visited**, and **a:hover** pseudoclasses.

17  Save index.html, and then test the links in your browser.

18  Close the browser and close index.html.

19  Open locations.html.

20  Delete the hotspot for Oregon.

21  Create polygon hotspots for Washington and California, as shown in Exhibit 6-1, and link them to their respective descriptions on that page.

22  Save locations.html and test the links in your browser.

23  Close the browser and all open files.

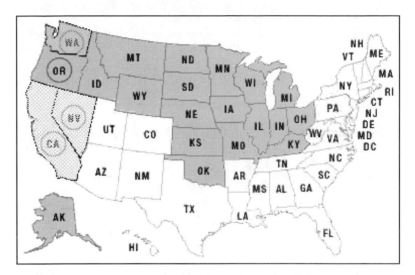

*Exhibit 6-1: Image maps for Washington and California after step 22*

## Review questions

1 A link with a Self target:

   A Opens in a new browser window.

   B Opens in an e-mail application.

   C Opens in the current browser window.

   D Opens in another browser window, only if another browser session is active.

2 A link with a Blank target:

   A Opens in a new browser window.

   B Opens in an e-mail application.

   C Opens in the current browser window.

   D Opens in another browser window, only if another browser session is active.

3 The clickable areas in an image map are referred to as:

   A Hotzones

   B Image link regions

   C Hotspots

   D Active areas

4 To create a link to a location within a document, you need to:

   A Create a local link on a page.

   B Create a named anchor, and then link to that anchor.

   C Create a link from one anchor to another.

   D Create a link to a page, and then on that page, create a link back to the original page.

5 The hover state is:

   A The default state of a link.

   B The state a link enters when you click it.

   C The state a link enters when you point to it.

   D The state a link enters when it has already been clicked.

# Unit 7
## Publishing

**Unit time: 45 minutes**

Complete this unit, and you'll know how to:

**A** Work with Map view, check file sizes and download times, check for broken links and orphaned files, cloak files, and validate code.

**B** Connect to a Web server with a secure FTP connection and upload and update a site.

# Topic A: Site checks

This topic covers the following Adobe ACE exam objectives for Dreamweaver CS3.

| # | Objective |
|---|-----------|
| 2.1 | Define a local site by using the Manage Sites dialog box. |
| 2.3 | Describe considerations related to case-sensitive links. |
| 2.6 | List and describe considerations related to designing a site for multiple platforms and browsers. |
| 3.18 | Discuss considerations related to naming conventions and case-sensitivity. |
| 4.4 | Transfer and synchronize files to and from a remote server. (Options include: Cloaking, background file transfer, Get, Put.) |
| 4.7 | Validate a site prior to deployment (Options include: link checking, accessibility checking, validating markup.) |

## Map view

*Explanation*

You can display your Web site in diagram form by using Map view, as shown in Exhibit 7-1. Map view displays the site pages and the link relationships among them, providing a complete view of your Web site's structure. Map view makes it easy to verify that your site's structure is set as you intend.

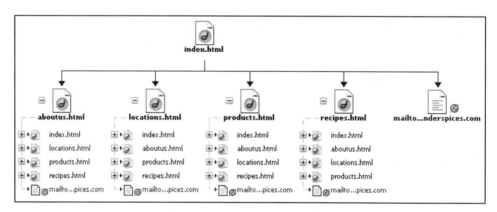

*Exhibit 7-1: An example of a site displayed in Map view*

To view the site map, the site must be defined in Dreamweaver. To switch to Map view, select Map view from the Site view list in the Files panel. By default, the site map is displayed within the Files panel, but you can expand it to fill the document window by clicking the Expand button on the right side of the panel. Some of the links in a site map might be colored blue or red. Blue links indicate external links (links to pages outside the current site), and red links indicate broken links.

### Site map preferences

You can make basic modifications to the site map by choosing options in the Site Map Layout category in the Site Definition dialog box. To open the dialog box, choose Site, Manage Sites. Then select the site with which you're working and click Edit. Select the Site Map Layout category, and then select the desired options.

### Advanced site options

Earlier, you learned how to define a site using the Site Definition wizard. Sometimes, however, you might want to specify other site options that aren't available in the wizard. The Advanced tab in the Site Definition dialog box provides more options for your sites, as shown in Exhibit 7-2. As you define a site, you can select from the categories on the left side and set the desired options.

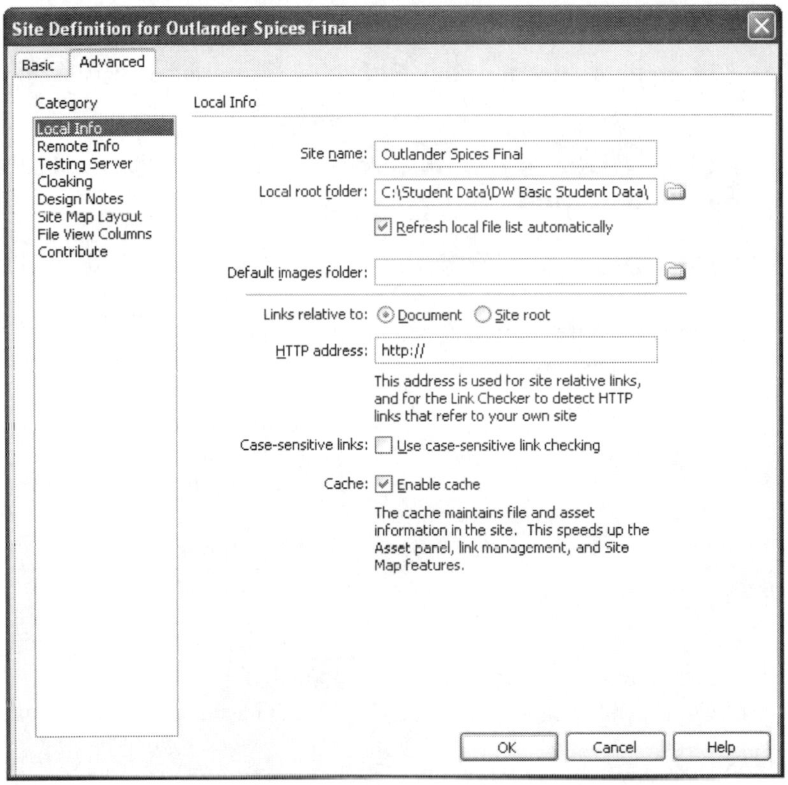

*Exhibit 7-2: The Advanced tab in the Site Definition dialog box*

### Case-sensitive link checking

The Case-sensitive links option, shown in Exhibit 7-2, ensures that your links work on a UNIX server where links are case-sensitive. If you're using a Windows or Mac server, this doesn't matter as much, but it's good practice to follow the strict naming and linking conventions of a UNIX system in case you ever need to store your site on a UNIX server.

## A-1: Exploring Map view

| Here's how | Here's why |
|---|---|
| 1 Choose **Site**, **New Site...** | To start the Site Definition Wizard. |
| 2 Activate the Advanced tab | |
| Enter **Outlander - Publishing** | (In the Site name box.) To name the Web site. |
| To the right of Local root folder, click ☐ | To open the "Choose local root folder" dialog box. |
| 3 Browse to the Outlander Spices folder | In the current unit folder. |
| Open the folder and click **Select** | To specify where the files for this site should be stored. |
| 4 Check **Use case-sensitive link checking** | To ensure that the links in the site work on a UNIX server. |
| Click **OK** | To define the site. You'll now view the site map. |
| 5 From the Site view list, select **Map view**, as shown | |
| | To display the Web site in Map view. The site map is visible in the Files panel. |
| 6 On the right side of the panel, click ☐ | To expand the site map to fill the application window. |
| Observe the site map | Only linked HTML pages appear. Other asset files in this directory, such as image or text files, aren't displayed. |

7  Next to aboutus.html, click ⊞

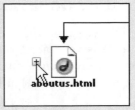

To show the pages linked to this page. In this page, there are five links, which correspond to the navigation bar. The last link is blue, indicating that it's an external link. In this case, it's a "mailto" link.

Expand the three remaining HTML pages

(The pages in the first row.) The locations page shows a red link, indicating that the link is broken. You'll fix this link later in this unit.

8  Choose **Site, Manage Sites...**

To open the Manage Sites dialog box.

Verify that Outlander - Publishing is selected, and click **Edit...**

To open the Site Definition dialog box.

9  Verify that the Advanced tab is active

You'll expand the site map to include dependent files.

In the Category column, select **Site Map Layout**

10  Next to Options, check **Display dependent files**

Click **OK**

To close the dialog box.

Click **Done**

To return to the site map. The map expands to show all the dependent files in the pages. This includes image files and style sheets.

11  Click 🖻

(At the top of the window.) To collapse the site map.

12  From the Site view list, select **Local view**

To return to the files listing.

## Testing page size and download time

*Explanation*

Before you upload a site, it's important to verify that your pages aren't too heavy, that is, excessively large, which causes pages to load slowly for many users. If your pages load slowly, some users, particularly those with slower connections, might leave your site and seek similar information or services elsewhere.

Dreamweaver calculates the size of an open document by counting up the kilobytes (K) of all text and linked objects, such as images and media files. You can view the download time of the current page at a particular connection speed on the right side of the status bar, as shown in Exhibit 7-3.

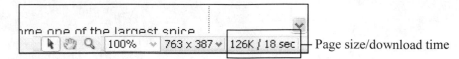

*Exhibit 7-3: The page size and download time in the status bar*

### Page size preferences

By default, the connection speed in the status bar is set to 56K, which is a slow baseline. You can change this setting in the Status Bar category in the Preferences dialog box.

*Do it!*

## A-2: Checking page size and download time

| Here's how | Here's why |
|---|---|
| 1 Open locations.html | From the Files panel. |
| Observe the page size and download time in the status bar | The page size is around 51K, and the download time on a 56K modem is about 8 seconds. |
| 2 Open aboutus.html | |
| In the status bar, observe the page size and download time | This page size is approximately 126K and will take about 18 seconds to load fully using a 56K modem. You'll change the connection speed standard, because you expect that nearly everyone in your target audience uses a faster connection than 56k. |
| 3 Choose **Edit**, **Preferences...** | To open the Preferences dialog box. |
| In the Category list, select **Status Bar** | To view status bar options. |
| From the Connection speed list, select **128** | Connection speed: [128 ▾] Kilobits per second |
| | To set a faster connection speed as the target baseline, closer to the slowest speed you expect most of your users to have. |
| Click **OK** | To close the dialog box. |
| 4 Observe the download time for the About Us page | At this faster connection speed, the page will load more quickly. Next, you'll check download times for users connecting at 700K, which is closer to what you expect most of your audience to use. |
| 5 Open the Preferences dialog box | Choose Edit, Preferences, or press Ctrl + U. |
| In the Connection speed box, type **700** | |
| Click **OK** | |
| 6 Observe the download time for the About Us page | For users connecting at 700K, the page will download in about 2 seconds. If you believe your target audience has slower connection speeds, consider optimizing all your images or reducing the number of images in use throughout your Web site. |
| 7 Close all open pages | |

## Broken links and orphaned files

*Explanation*

Before you publish a Web site, you should verify that all the links in the site work correctly. As you build pages, it's often easy to mistype a link, or accidentally link to a page that was later deleted or renamed. If users were to click these broken links, they would likely be presented with an error indicating that the browser can't locate the linked page. Having to open each file and test every link would be a time-consuming and tedious development task. Fortunately, Dreamweaver can check the integrity of all your local and external links for you.

To check links for an entire site:

1   In the Files panel, select a Web site.

2   Right-click in the Files panel and choose Check Links, Entire Local Site. You can also choose Site, Check Links Sitewide, or press Ctrl+F8.

3   In the Results panel, you can identify and repair broken links, as shown in Exhibit 7-4.

4   From the Show list, select External Links to review all external links.

5   From the Show list, select Orphaned Files to display any orphaned files that might exist in your site.

| ▼ **Results** | Search | Reference | Validation | Target Browser Check | Link Checker |
|---|---|---|---|---|---|
| Show: | Broken Links ⌄ | (links to files not found on local disk) | | | |

| Files | Broken Links |
|---|---|
| /products.html | locatoins.html |

33 Total, 6 HTML, 1 Orphaned  72 All links, 67 OK, 1 Broken, 4 External

*Exhibit 7-4: The Link Checker in the Results panel group*

### Orphaned files

You can also check for *orphaned files*, which are files that reside in your site folders but have no pages linking to them. These files might include early drafts of Web pages or image files that you decided not to use. Removing orphaned files from your site before uploading prevents unnecessary bloat on the server and make site maintenance easier.

### Cloaking

Sometimes you might have orphaned files that you don't want to remove from the site. For example, you might have text documents or original image files, such as those in Photoshop .psd format, that you might want to access later. Keeping them with the site folder makes them easier to locate.

Cloaking folders or file types allows you to store them in your site, but keeps them from being included in normal site operations, such as link reports or uploading functions. To cloak a folder, right-click the folder and choose Cloaking, Cloak. Cloaked folders and documents appear with a red line through them, as shown in Exhibit 7-5.

*Exhibit 7-5: The Files panel showing cloaked folders and files*

To cloak file types, right-click in the Files panel and choose Cloaking, Settings to open the Site Definition dialog box. In the Cloaking category, check Cloak files ending with, and then enter the file extensions you want to cloak.

## A-3: Checking links and cloaking files

| Here's how | Here's why |
|---|---|
| 1 Right-click in the Files panel and choose **Check Links**, **Entire Local Site** | The Results panel group appears with the Link Checker panel activated. |
| Observe the Broken Links list | A broken link appears in the list. In this case, a spelling error in the file name breaks the link. |
| 2 Under Broken Links, click **locatoins.html** | |
| | You'll correct the misspelling of the file name. |
| Type **locations.html** | To enter the correct file name for the linked file. |
| Press (↵ ENTER) | The file no longer appears in the Broken Links list. |
| 3 From the Show list, select **External Links** | To view the external links in this site's pages. These links don't indicate errors; they're listed here for reference only. |
| 4 From the Show list, select **Orphaned Files** | Several files appear that aren't linked to any pages in the site. You'll remove the image files. However, because you might need the text files later, you'll cloak those specific file types. |
| 5 In the Files panel, expand the images subfolder | |
| Click the chilis.jpg image and press (DELETE) | To delete the unused image. |
| 6 Delete the greenbar.gif image | Select the image and press Delete. |
| Collapse the images subfolder | |
| 7 In the Files panel, right-click one of the text files and choose **Cloaking**, **Settings** | To open the Site Definition dialog box. |
| 8 Check **Cloak files ending with** | |

9 Edit the box to read **.doc .txt**, as shown

> ☑ Cloak files ending with:
>
> .doc .txt|

Click **OK**    A dialog box appears, indicating that the cache for the site will be recreated.

Click **OK**    The two text documents now have a red line across them, indicating they're cloaked and won't be uploaded with the rest of the site.

## HTML validation

*Explanation*
Before you upload your site, you should also check to ensure that your code meets compliance standards. The World Wide Web Consortium (W3C) establishes coding standards. If there are code errors in your pages, they might display incorrectly in some browsers.

You can validate the code in certain pages or for all the pages in a local site. To validate the code for a page, open the page, and choose File, Validate, Markup. The Validation panel in the Results panel group becomes active and any errors are listed, as shown in Exhibit 7-6. To validate the code for an entire site, click the Validate button on the left side of the panel, and choose Validate Entire Current Local Site.

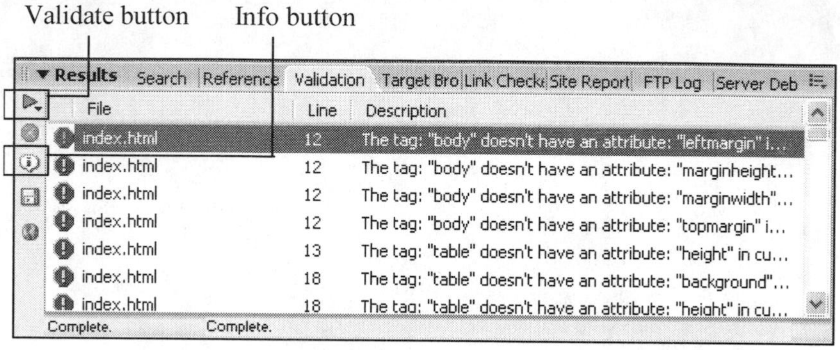

*Exhibit 7-6: The Validation panel in the Results panel group*

To fix errors, double-click the error in the Validation panel. When you do so, the page activates in Split view, and the corresponding code is highlighted. Fix the code, and that item no longer appears in the list of errors. You can reference additional information about the error by clicking the Info button on the left side of the panel.

To find additional information about W3C guidelines, you can visit the W3C site at http://www.w3.org. You can use their site to find information about changes or additions to the current guidelines and find specific information about certain tags, such as which ones are deprecated. A *deprecated* tag is one that has been outdated in favor of new elements or CSS.

*Do it!*

### A-4: Validating code

| Here's how | Here's why |
|---|---|
| 1 Open index.html | You'll validate the code for this page. |
| 2 Choose **File, Validate, Markup** | The Validation panel in the Results panel group becomes active and lists one error. It refers to the background image applied to one of the table cells. This attribute isn't valid for table cells by XHTML standards, which Dreamweaver uses by default. You need to remove the background image in order for the code to be considered valid XHTML. |
| 3 Double-click the error | To view the element in the layout. The selected table cell uses the home_bg.jpg image as a background. |
| 4 In the Property inspector, delete the file path in the Bg box | Because the cell has a similar background color applied to it, the change in the layout is subtle. |
| 5 On the left side of the Validation panel, click 🔻 | To show the button list. |
| From the list, select **Validate Current Document** | The panel now shows that there are no validation errors. |
| 6 Click 🔻 | To show the button list. |
| From the list, select **Validate Entire Current Local Site** | There are no other errors in the site. |
| 7 Close the Results panel | |
| 8 Save and close index.html | |

# Topic B: Web site publishing

This topic covers the following Adobe ACE exam objectives for Dreamweaver CS3.

| # | Objective |
|---|-----------|
| 1.4 | List and describe the features and functionality of ftp and how it is used in Dreamweaver. |
| 2.6 | List and describe considerations related to designing a site for multiple platforms and browsers. |
| 3.18 | Discuss considerations related to naming conventions and case-sensitivity. |
| 4.2 | List and describe the different methods for accessing a remote site. (Methods include: FTP, LAN, VSS, WebDAV.) |
| 4.3 | Given an access method, configure site definitions. |
| 4.4 | Transfer and synchronize files to and from a remote server. (Options include: Cloaking, background file transfer, Get, Put.) |
| 4.5 | Manage assets, links, and files for a site. |
| 4.6 | Configure preferences, and explain the process required to compare files. |

## Publishing basics

*Explanation*

You publish a Web site by copying the site files from your local PC to a remote Web server. A *Web server* is a computer configured with Web server software and the Internet protocols required to serve pages and other resources upon request. Dreamweaver makes it easy to set publishing parameters for your site and to transfer your site files to a Web server.

A Web server is connected to the Internet via an *Internet service provider* (ISP) or a *hosting center*. The ISP or hosting center provides disk space for Web site files, as well as other services, such as site promotion.

### Domain names

A *domain name* serves as both the name and address of your site. Your ISP can help you select and register a domain name. A domain name, such as outlanderspices.com, for example, is easy for users to remember, immediately identifies the company, and is fairly easy to type into a browser's address bar.

**File names**

Sometimes the way you name your files can cause problems when you upload the site to a server. For example, you might upload your pages to a UNIX server, which uses different file path protocols. To create file names that comply with just about any operating system, follow these guidelines:

- Keep file names short. For ease of maintenance on the site, the file name should describe the file's content or function.
- Don't include spaces in the name. To separate words, use the underscore character; for example, *product_list.html*.
- Don't use any characters other than letters, numerals, and the underscore.
- Always start file names with a letter.
- Treat uppercase and lowercase letters as separate characters. For example, your server might not consider aboutus.html and AboutUs.html to be the same file. A good way to keep from running into problems is to use only lowercase letters.

## Server connections

Before you can upload files to a Web server, you must first establish a connection between your PC and the server.

**Methods for accessing a remote site**

SFTP (Secure File Transfer Protocol) is a popular method of transferring files. It uses FTP, the standard file transfer protocol, and combines it with authentication and encryption protocols to protect the transmission.

WebDAV (Web-based Distributed Authoring and Versioning) is a set of extensions to the HTTP protocol that allow users to edit and manage files collaboratively on remote Web servers.

Dreamweaver can also transfer data between servers located on a LAN (Local Area Network), and can transfer data using Microsoft technologies, such as the version control application VSS (Visual SourceSafe) and RDS (Remote Data Services).

Before setting up a server connection, check with your ISP to make sure that the Web server supports the connection protocol you want to use. If it does, the ISP typically provides information for connecting to the server. This information includes the FTP host name, the host directory, and a login name and password.

**Security**

The Internet isn't a secure environment. When you transfer files to a remote machine, the information isn't sent directly to that machine. Instead, it's usually routed through several machines to get to its destination. Anyone along the route can access what you're sending, including your username and password. If this information falls into the wrong hands, your account and the remote site to which you have access might no longer be secure.

Securing file transfers usually involves encrypting the files with an encryption protocol, such as the SSH (Secure Shell protocol) or SSL (Secure Socket Layer). Dreamweaver supports these protocols automatically when you connect to a server using SFTP or WebDAV.

**Setting site definitions**

To configure site definitions for a specific access method:

1 Choose Site, Manage Sites. The Manage Sites dialog box appears.

2 Select the site to be configured and click Edit. The Site Definition wizard appears.

3 Activate the Advanced tab.

4 Under Category, select Remote Info.

5 From the Access list, select the method to connect to the remote Web server, as shown in Exhibit 7-7.

6 Under Category, select Testing Server, if necessary.

7 From the Server model list, select the server model used for your database connection or dynamic Web page, if necessary.

8 From the Access list, select the method to connect to the testing server.

9 Click OK to close the Site Definitions wizard.

10 Click Done to close the Manage Sites dialog box.

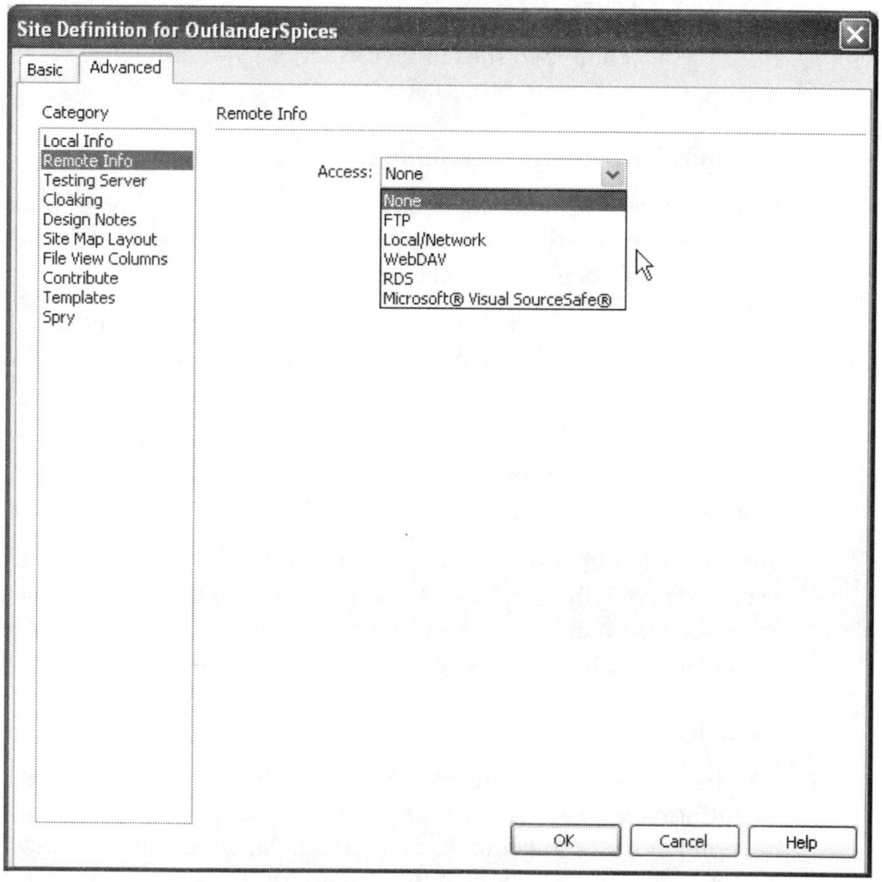

*Exhibit 7-7: Access method site definitions*

*Do it!*

## B-1: Connecting to a server using secure FTP

| Here's how | Here's why |
|---|---|
| 1 Choose **Site, Manage Sites...** | To open the Manage Sites dialog box. You'll explore the settings for secure FTP connection. |
| 2 Verify that Outlander - Publishing is selected, and click **Edit...** | The Site Definition Wizard appears. You'll explore the steps required to connect to a server through a secure FTP connection. |
| 3 Activate the Advanced tab | If necessary. |
| Under Category, select **Remote Info** | To display the remote connection options. |
| 4 From the Access list, select **FTP** | This page of the wizard is context-sensitive. When you select FTP as the remote connection type, additional fields appear. |
| 5 In the FTP host box, enter **ftp.outlanderspices.com** | To specify the address of an FTP host where you will send files. |
| 6 In the Host directory box, enter the path to the Test Site folder | (In the current unit folder.) The Host directory specifies the path to the remote site. |
| 7 In the Login box, enter your first name | For a real site, the hosting center administrator would typically assign a user name. |
| 8 In the Password box, enter **password** | For a real site, the hosting center administrator would typically assign a password. |
| 9 Check **Use Secure FTP (SFTP)** | |

Access: FTP
FTP host: ftp.outlanderspices.com
Host directory: C:\Student Data\Unit_07\Test Site
Login: Lee          Test
Password: ●●●●●●●●  ☑ Save
☐ Use passive FTP
☐ Use IPv6 transfer mode
☐ Use firewall          Firewall
☑ Use Secure FTP (SFTP)

To encrypt file transfers and guard access to your files, user names, and passwords. The Web server must be an SFTP server.

| 10 Click **Cancel** | To close the wizard. |
| Click **Done** | To close the Manage Sites dialog box. |

## Site publishing

*Explanation*

When you upload files to a Web server, the local folder where the site resides on your PC is automatically duplicated on the Web server. All files and subfolders are copied, except those that have cloaking applied to them. You can also publish a site to another location on your local PC, either as practice or because your PC is acting as the Web server.

To upload a site, perform a *put*, as follows:

1   Define the Web site.

2   Connect to the remote site.

3   Upload a site or a folder using the following methods:

- To upload an entire site, select the root site folder in the Files panel, and then click the Put File(s) button.

- To upload a subfolder within the site, select the subfolder in the Files panel, and then click the Put File(s) button.

In addition, you can expand the Files panel to display additional options for uploading a site or a subfolder within a site. To do so, click the Expand/Collapse button, to expand the Files panel, and do either of the following:

- To upload an entire site, drag the root site folder from the Local Files pane to the Remote Site pane.

- To upload a subfolder within the site, drag the subfolder from the Local Files pane to the Remote Site pane.

### Background file transfers

While your site is uploading, you can perform other non-server-related activities, such as editing pages or style sheets or generating site reports. When the transfer is complete, you can update the remote site with any changes by synchronizing it with the local site.

### Synchronization

Dreamweaver synchronizes your local and remote sites using the time stamps saved with the documents. So, if you edit and save a page on the local site, it has a more recent time stamp than the page on the server. To see which files are newer on the local site, right-click in the Files panel and choose Select, Newer Local. To see which files on the remote server are newer, choose Select, Newer Remote.

To synchronize the local and remote sites, right-click in the Files panel and choose Synchronize. You can also choose Site, Synchronize. Dreamweaver then automatically compares the time stamps of the two sites and updates the site containing the older pages with the newer ones.

*Do it!*    **B-2:   Uploading a site**

| Here's how | Here's why |
|---|---|
| 1  Open the Manage Sites dialog box | Choose Site, Manage Sites. |
| Click **Edit...** | You'll practice uploading a site by transferring the site to a folder on your PC. |
| Under Category, select **Remote Info** | To display the remote connection options. |
| 2  In the Access list, select **Local/Network** | This page of the Site Definition Wizard is context-sensitive. When you select Local/Network as the remote connection type, additional fields appear. |
| 3  Click 🗀 | The Browse button. |
| In the current unit folder, open the Test Site folder | |
| Click **Open** | |
| Click **Select** | To specify this as the remote folder. |
| 4  Click **OK** | The Adobe Dreamweaver CS3 dialog box appears. |
| Click **OK** | To confirm that a cache will be recreated and to close the dialog box and wizard. |
| Click **Done** | To close the Manage Sites dialog box. |
| 5  In the Files panel, click 🗗 | The Expand/Collapse button. |
| 6  Click ▤ | (The Site Files button is at the top of the window.) To view the files in the remote folder and the files in the local folder. |
| Click ↻ | (The Refresh button.) To refresh the panel and display the remote folder. Because there's nothing in the folder yet, only the folder icon is visible. |
| 7  In the Local Files pane, select the root folder, as shown | |
| | You'll upload the entire site. |

| | |
|---|---|
| 8 Click ⬆ | (The Put File(s) button.) To upload the site files from the local folder to the remote folder. A dialog box appears, asking if you're sure you want to put the entire site. |
| Click **OK** | To put (upload) the entire site to the remote folder. |
| Observe the folders in both panes | Both panes contain the same folders and files, except for the files you cloaked earlier. |
| 9 Click 🖽 | (The Expand/Collapse button.) To collapse the Files panel. |

## Site updating

*Explanation*

When you edit the content or design of a particular Web page, you can update that specific file on the Web server. Sometimes, before updating a specific file, you might wish to perform a *get* first, to download the version of the file that's currently on the Web server.

To perform a get:

1  Connect to the remote site.
2  Download files or folders using the following methods:

- To download an entire site, select the root site folder in the Files panel, and then click the Get File(s) button.
- To download a specific file, select the file in the Files panel, and then click the Get File(s) button.

In addition, you can expand the Files panel to display more options for downloading a site or a specific file. To do so, click the Expand/Collapse button to expand the Files panel and do either of the following:

- To download an entire site, drag the root site folder from the Remote Files pane to the Local Site pane.
- To download a specific file from the site, drag the file from the Remote Files pane to the Local Site pane.

To put a specific file, select that file and click the Put Files(s) button, or drag it to the Remote Files pane.

### Dependent files

When you get or put a file, Dreamweaver can prompt you to include that file's dependent files. Dependent files include assets and files, such as images, style sheets, and any other files that are referenced by the file being put and which may have been altered or updated.

To enable or disable prompting, choose Edit, Preferences. Under Category, select Site. Check or clear the Dependent files options, as shown in Exhibit 7-8.

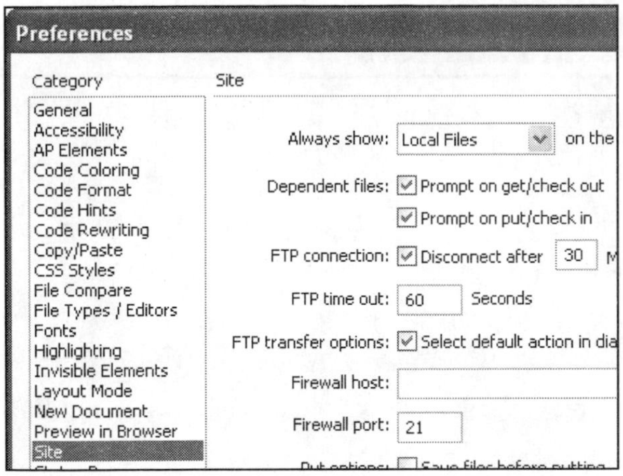

*Exhibit 7-8: The options in the Site category of the Preferences dialog box*

### Compare files

If you try to put a file to the server, Dreamweaver prompts you, if the local file being put is different from the remote file. If you've installed a third-party file comparison application, you can launch that application from within Dreamweaver. If you perform a brief Web search, you'll see that there are a vast number of file comparison applications (such as WinMerge) that are available for download from various free or pay sites. To set preferences for Dreamweaver's Compare function:

1   Install a third-party file comparison application according to the manufacturer's instructions.

2   Choose Edit, Preferences. The Preferences dialog box appears.

3   Under Category, choose File Compare.

4   Click Browse. The Select External Editor dialog box appears.

5   Navigate to the application you installed.

6   Click Open to select the application and close the dialog box.

7   Click OK to close the Preferences dialog box.

To compare files:

1   In the Files panel, select a local file.

2   Right-click and choose Compare with Remote. Dreamweaver launches the third-party file comparison application, which compares the two files.

3   Observe the differences between the local and remote files, then close the application.

*Do it!*  **B-3:   Updating a site**

## Questions and answers

1  What's a get?

2  What's a put?

3  How does Dreamweaver help you to manage assets and files?

4  How do you enable or disable dependent file prompting?

5  What file comparison features does Dreamweaver offer natively?

6  How do you specify an installed file comparison application in Dreamweaver?

# Unit summary: Publishing

**Topic A**

In this topic, you learned how to perform several checks on a completed site. You learned how to use **Map view**, which allows you to view an entire site structure quickly. You checked the **file size and download times** for site pages, and you ran a site report to find any **broken links** or **orphaned files**. Lastly, you learned how to **validate the code** in your pages against W3C guidelines.

**Topic B**

In this topic, you learned the basics of **Web site publishing** with Dreamweaver. You learned how to connect to a server using **SFTP**, and you learned how to **upload a site** to a local or remote folder. Then, you learned how to update a site by transferring one or more files with a **get** or a **put**. You learned that Dreamweaver can prompt you to include **dependent files** with the get or put, and that Dreamweaver can launch a third-party file comparison application, if you have one installed.

## Independent practice activity

In this activity, you'll define a Web site, check for broken links and orphaned files, and practice uploading a Web site by uploading it to a local folder.

1 Define a new Web site, titled **Outlander Publishing Practice**, using the Outlander Spices Practice folder.

2 Check the links in the site. (*Hint*: In the Files panel, right-click the site and choose Check Links, Entire Local Site.)

3 Repair the broken link that was caused by a typo.

4 Delete the orphaned files.

5 Close the Results panel group.

6 Establish a connection to the Test Site folder within the Practice subfolder. (*Hint:* Choose Site, Manage Sites. Click Edit. In the Remote Info category, choose Local/Network. Navigate to the Test Site folder, and then click OK.)

7 View both the local files and the remote Test Site folder. (*Hint:* In the Files panel, click the Expand/Collapse button and, if necessary, click the Site Files button to view the local folder and the remote folder.)

8 Upload the entire site to the remote folder. (*Hint:* In the Local Files pane, select the root folder, then click the Put File(s) button.)

9 Collapse the Files panel, and close Dreamweaver.

## Review questions

1   In Map view, what do blue links indicate?

   A   Anchors

   B   Image map links

   C   Broken links

   D   External links

2   In the Advanced tab in the Site Definition dialog box, what does the Case-sensitive links option do?

   A   Ensures that your links work on a Unix server.

   B   Configures Dreamweaver to produce a warning box when you link to files that use uppercase letters.

   C   Requires linked files to include at least one uppercase letter in the file name.

   D   Requires linked files to consist of only lowercase letters in the file name.

3   How can you change the connection speed with which Dreamweaver calculates download time?

   A   Select a new connection speed from the Page size/download time list in the status bar.

   B   Right-click the Page size/download time list in the status bar, then choose a new connection speed.

   C   Open the Page Properties dialog box, select the Title/Encoding category, and select a new connection speed from the Connection speed list.

   D   Open the Preferences dialog box, select the Status bar category, and select a new connection speed from the Connection speed list.

4   How can you check links sitewide? [Choose all that apply.]

   A   Press Ctrl+F8.

   B   Right-click the Files panel and choose Check Links, Entire Local Site.

   C   Choose Site, Check Links Sitewide.

   D   Select a file in the Files panel, and click Check Links Sitewide in the Property Inspector.

5  How can you cloak specific file types?

  A  In the Files panel, right-click a file that you want to cloak, then select Cloak File Type.

  B  Open the Preferences dialog box and select the File Types/Editors category. Check Cloak files ending with, and enter the file extensions you want to cloak.

  C  Right-click the Files panel and choose Cloaking, Settings. In the Cloaking category, check Cloak files ending with, and enter the file extensions you want to cloak.

  D  Choose Site, Advanced, Cloak files ending with. In the dialog box, enter the file extensions you want to cloak.

6  How can you validate the code for a page?

  A  Choose File, Validate, Markup.

  B  Choose Site, Check Links Sitewide.

  C  In the Files panel, right-click the file, then choose Check Page, Validate Markup.

  D  Switch to Code View, then choose Commands, Clean Up XHTML.

7  What's a deprecated tag?

  A  A tag that's nested inside another tag.

  B  A tag that can't have any attributes applied to it.

  C  A tag whose use is discouraged in favor of newer methods.

  D  A tag that has other tags nested inside it.

8  Which of the following are important guidelines to consider when naming site files? [Choose all that apply.]

  A  Keep file names as short and meaningful as possible.

  B  Start file names with a number.

  C  Start file names with a letter.

  D  Don't include spaces in the file names.

  E  Don't use special characters other than the underscore.

  F  Separate words in the file names with one space only.

9  Which are ways you can connect to a server? [Choose all that apply.]

  A  FTP

  B  SFTP

  C  XML

  D  WebDAV

10  Which encryption protocols does Dreamweaver support? [Choose all that apply.]

    A  AOL

    B  SOL

    C  SSL

    D  SSH

11  How can you synchronize the local and remote sites? [Choose all that apply.]

    A  Choose Site, Synchronize.

    B  In the Files panel, click the Refresh button.

    C  Choose File, Check Page, Check Accessibility.

    D  Right-click in the Files panel and choose Synchronize.

12  After you connect to a remote server, how can you upload an individual file? [Choose all that apply.]

    A  Select the file in the Files panel and click the Put File(s) button.

    B  In the Files panel, select the folder in which the file is located and click the Put File(s) button.

    C  Expand the Files panel, then drag the folder in which the file is located from the Local Files pane to the Remote Site pane.

    D  Expand the Files panel, then drag the file from the Local Files pane to the Remote Site pane.

# Appendix A
## ACE exam objectives map

This appendix provides the following information:

**A** ACE exam objectives for Dreamweaver CS3 with references to corresponding coverage in ILT Series courseware.

# Topic A: ACE exam objectives

*Explanation*      The following table lists the Adobe Certified Expert (ACE) exam objectives for Dreamweaver CS3 and indicates where each objective is covered in conceptual explanations, hands-on activities, or both.

| # | Objective | Course level | Conceptual information | Supporting activities |
|---|---|---|---|---|
| 1.1 | Given an HTML tag, explain the purpose of that tag. (Tags include: <div> <span> <table> <a>.) | Basic | Unit 1, Topic D | D-1 |
| 1.2 | Describe the difference between CSS classes and IDs. | Basic | Unit 3, Topic C | C-1 |
| | | Advanced | Unit 1, Topic B | B-5 |
| 1.3 | Explain how JavaScript is used on the client in Web pages. | Advanced | Unit 4, Topic A | A-1 |
| 1.4 | List and describe the features and functionality of ftp and how it is used in Dreamweaver. | Basic | Unit 7, Topic B | B-1 |
| 2.1 | Define a local site by using the Manage Sites dialog box. | Basic | Unit 7, Topic A | A-1 |
| 2.2 | Manage site definitions for local, remote, and testing server information. | Basic | Unit 2, Topic A | A-1 |
| 2.3 | Describe considerations related to case-sensitive links. | Basic | Unit 7, Topic A | A-1 |
| 2.4 | Given a scenario, define the structure of a site. | Basic | Unit 2, Topic A | A-1 |
| 2.5 | Given a scenario, select and set the appropriate resolution for a site. | Basic | Unit 2, Topic B | B-1 |
| 2.6 | List and describe considerations related to designing a site for multiple platforms and browsers. | Basic | Unit 1, Topic C<br>Unit 2, Topic A<br>Unit 7, Topic A<br>Unit 7, Topic B | C-5<br>A-1<br>A-1 |
| 2.7 | List and describe the features Dreamweaver provides for Accessibility Standards/Section 508 compliance. | Basic | Unit 1, Topic C<br>Unit 4, Topic A<br>Unit 5, Topic A | C-4<br>A-1<br>A-3 |
| | | Advanced | Unit 3, Topic B<br>Unit 8, Topic C | B-2<br>C-1 |
| 2.8 | Explain how templates are used to architect for reuse and consistency. | Advanced | Unit 2, Topic C | C-1, C-2 |
| 2.9 | Create pages by using CSS starter pages. | Basic | Unit 2, Topic B<br>Unit 3, Topic C | C-1 |

| # | Objective | Course level | Conceptual information | Supporting activities |
|---|-----------|--------------|------------------------|------------------------|
| 2.10 | Explain how to extend Dreamweaver by using Extensions. | Advanced | Unit 4, Topic B | B-4 |
| 2.11 | Given a scenario, set development Preferences. | Basic | Unit 1, Topic C<br>Unit 2, Topic A<br>Unit 2, Topic B<br>Unit 3, Topic A | <br>A-1<br><br>A-1 |
| 2.12 | Given a scenario, choose the proper method to lay out a page. (Methods include: tables, layers, CSS Box model.) | Basic<br><br>Advanced | Unit 4, Topic A<br><br>Unit 1, Topic B<br>Unit 3, Topic A<br>Unit 5, Topic A | <br><br>B-1<br>A-1<br>A-1 |
| 3.1 | List and describe how to navigate the Dreamweaver UI. | Basic | Unit 1, Topic B | B-1 thru B-3 |
| 3.2 | Use Find and Replace including support for regular expressions. | Basic | Unit 1, Topic A | A-1 |
| 3.3 | Create and use page templates. | Advanced | Unit 2, Topic C | C-1, C-2 |
| 3.4 | Create and maintain Cascading Style Sheets (CSS.) | Basic<br><br>Advanced | Unit 3, Topic C<br>Unit 6, Topic C<br><br>Unit 1, Topic A<br>Unit 1, Topic B | C-1 thru C-5<br>C-1<br><br>A-1<br>B-2 thru B-5 |
| 3.5 | Create and use reusable page objects by using library items. | Advanced | Unit 2, Topic A | A-1, A-2 |
| 3.6 | Explain the purpose of and how to use Server-side includes. | Advanced | Unit 2, Topic B | B-1, B-2, B-3 |
| 3.7 | Create and use code Snippets. | Advanced | Unit 2, Topic A | A-1 |
| 3.8 | Given a method, lay out a page. (Methods include: Table Layout, Layers, Expanded Tables mode.) | Basic<br><br>Advanced | Unit 4, Topic A<br>Unit 4, Topic D<br><br>Unit 5, Topic A<br>Unit 5, Topic B | A-1<br>D-1, D-2, D-3<br><br>A-1<br>B-1, B-2, B-3 |
| 3.9 | List and describe the options for creating and saving new pages. | Basic | Unit 2, Topic B | B-1 |
| 3.10 | Set document properties by using the Document Properties dialog box. | Basic | Unit 2, Topic B | B-3, B-4 |
| 3.11 | Lay out a page by using guides. | Advanced | Unit 5, Topic A | A-1 |
| 3.12 | List and describe the options available for formatting the structure of a document. (Options include: paragraph breaks, line breaks, non-breaking spaces, tables.) | Basic | Unit 3, Topic A<br>Unit 4, Topic A<br>Unit 4, Topic B | A-1, A-2<br>A-1, A-2<br>B-2 |
| 3.13 | List and describe, and resolve issues related to, browser compatibility. | Advanced | Unit 8, Topic B | B-1, B-2 |

| # | Objective | Course level | Conceptual information | Supporting activities |
|---|-----------|--------------|------------------------|-----------------------|
| 3.14 | Use JavaScript behaviors to implement page functionality. (Behaviors include: Pop-Up Menus, Open Browser Window, Swap Image, Go To URL.) | Advanced | Unit 4, Topic B | B-1, B-2, B-3 |
| 3.15 | Add Flash elements to a Web page. (Options include: text, buttons, video, paper.) | Advanced | Unit 6, Topic A<br>Unit 6, Topic B | A-1, A-2<br>B-1, B-2, B-3 |
| 3.16 | List and describe the functionality provided by Dreamweaver for XML. | Advanced | Unit 7, Topic A<br>Unit 7, Topic B | A-1, A-2<br>B-1, B-2, B-3 |
| 3.17 | Given a coding tool or feature, describe the purpose of or how to use that tool or feature. (Tools or features include: Code and Design View, Code Collapse, Code Navigation, Code Hinting, Coding Context Menu option.) | Basic<br><br><br>Advanced | Unit 1, Topic D<br>Unit 3, Topic A<br><br>Unit 4, Topic A | D-1<br>A-2<br><br>A-1 |
| 3.18 | Discuss considerations related to naming conventions and case sensitivity (e.g., variations between UNIX and Windows.) | Basic | Unit 7, Topic A<br>Unit 7, Topic B | A-1 |
| 3.19 | Annotate files by using Design Notes and Comments | Advanced | Unit 8, Topic A | A-2 |
| 4.1 | Manage collaboration with multiple developers by using Check In-Check Out. | Advanced | Unit 8, Topic A | A-1 |
| 4.2 | List and describe the different methods for accessing a remote site. (Methods include: FTP, LAN, VSS, WebDAV.) | Basic | Unit 7, Topic B | B-1 |
| 4.3 | Given an access method, configure site definitions. | Basic | Unit 7, Topic B | B-1 |
| 4.4 | Transfer and synchronize files to and from a remote server. (Options include: Cloaking, background file transfer, Get, Put.) | Basic | Unit 7, Topic A<br>Unit 7, Topic B | A-3<br>B-2, B-3 |
| 4.5 | Manage assets, links, and files for a site. | Basic | Unit 7, Topic B | B-3 |
| 4.6 | Configure preferences, and explain the process required to compare files. | Basic<br><br>Advanced | Unit 7, Topic B<br><br>Unit 8, Topic A | B-3 |
| 4.7 | Validate a site prior to deployment (Options include: link checking, accessibility checking, validating markup.) | Basic<br><br>Advanced | Unit 7, Topic A<br><br>Unit 8, Topic C | A-3, A-4<br><br>C-1 |

# Course summary

This summary contains information to help you bring the course to a successful conclusion. Using this information, you'll be able to:

**A** Use the summary text to reinforce what you've learned in class.

**B** Determine the next courses in this series, if any, as well as any other resources that might help you continue to learn about Dreamweaver CS3.

# Topic A: Course summary

Use the following summary text to reinforce what you've learned in class.

## Unit summaries

### Unit 1

In this unit, you learned the basics of the Internet and HTML. You identified the main components of the **Dreamweaver interface** and learned how to customize the workspace. You performed basic Web page editing by adding and **formatting text** and images, and you applied basic **font styles** and previewed a Web page in a browser. Finally, you learned about **HTML tags**, including basic structural tags, and you performed some basic tasks in **Code view**.

### Unit 2

In this unit, you learned some basic concepts for **planning a Web site**. You defined a Web site, and you learned how to work with the **Files panel** and the **Assets panel**. Then you created Web pages, imported text from documents, and set **page properties**, including page and text color.

### Unit 3

In this unit, you **converted line breaks to paragraph breaks** to separate text into paragraphs, and you inserted **special characters and non-breaking spaces**. You also learned the basics of **document structure**, and created **ordered** and **unordered lists**. Then you learned the basics of **Cascading Style Sheets (CSS)** and created and applied **element styles**, **class styles**, and **pseudo-element styles**.

### Unit 4

In this unit, you created and formatted **tables** and **nested tables**, **inserted rows** and **columns,** set row and column properties, and applied **background color** to cells. You also applied **fixed and variable widths**, **aligned content in cells**, and **modified cell borders** and **cell padding**. Finally, you used a **layout table and layout cells** to arrange page content.

### Unit 5

In this unit, you learned about the **GIF, JPEG**, and **PNG** image file formats. Then you learned the advantages and disadvantages of using **image-based text**. You modified image tag attributes, applied image **backgrounds**, and finally, you learned how to write effective **alternate text**.

### Unit 6

In this unit, you created **links** to other pages and resources, and you created **named anchors** and **e-mail links**. Then you created an **image map** and drew **hotspots** using various **shape tools**. Finally, you learned about the four **link states** and applied CSS styles to each state.

**Unit 7**

In this unit, you performed several checks on a completed site. You learned how to use **Map view** to verify a site's structure, check the **file size** and **download times** for site pages, and run a **site report** to find any **broken links** or **orphaned files**. You also learned how to **cloak files** and **validate code**. Lastly, you learned how to **connect to a server** using SFTP and to **upload a site** to a local or remote folder.

# Topic B: Continued learning after class

It's impossible to learn to use any software effectively in a single day. To get the most out of this class, you should begin working with Dreamweaver CS3 to perform real tasks as soon as possible. We also offer resources for continued learning.

## Next courses in this series

This is the first course in this series. The next course in this series is:

- *Dreamweaver CS3: Advanced, ACE Edition*

## Other resources

For more information, visit www.axzopress.com.

# Dreamweaver CS3: Basic

## Quick reference

| Button | Shortcut keys | Function |
|---|---|---|
| | | Hides the panel groups and expands the document window. |
| | CTRL + TAB | Expands the Property inspector. |
| | | Hides the Property inspector and expands the document window. |
| I | CTRL + I | Makes the selected text italic. |
| | F12 | Previews the current page in a browser. |
| Split | | Splits the document window into Code view and Design view. |
| Code | | Switches to Code view. |
| Design | | Switches to Design view. |
| | | Opens a dialog box where you can browse to a folder. |
| | | Expands and collapses the Files panel. |
| | | Expands a tree in the Files panel or in Map view. |
| | | Attaches an External Style Sheet to the current page. |
| All | | Displays all style-sheet files in the CSS panel. |
| | | Opens a style definition (from the CSS panel) for editing. |
| | CTRL + ALT + T | Inserts an HTML table when you drag from the button to the document window. |

| Button | Shortcut keys | Function |
|---|---|---|
| **B** | `CTRL` + `B` | Makes the selected text bold. |
| | `CTRL` + `ALT` + `SHIFT` + `R` | Aligns the selected text or object to the right. |
| | | Begins a layout table. |
| | | Begins a layout cell. |
| | | Resets a modified image to its original size and proportions. |
| | `CTRL` + `ALT` + `A` | Inserts a named anchor in the document. |
| | | Draws a rectangular or square hotspot on an image. |
| | | Draws a polygon hotspot on an image. |
| | `F5` | Refreshes the view in the Files panel. |
| | `CTRL` + `SHIFT` + `U` | Uploads site files from the local folder to a remote folder. |

# Glossary

**Assets**

The components of your Web site, such as images and multimedia files.

**Cell padding**

The amount of space between a cell border and the cell content.

**Class styles**

Types of styles that you can use to give names to your HTML elements. These allow you to define elements and page sections specifically, rather than relying on the default HTML tag names. Class styles can be used multiple times in a document.

**Definition list**

An HTML list for structuring terms and their corresponding definitions. Often used for glossaries, pages of frequently asked questions (FAQs), and similar contexts.

**Deprecated tags**

Tags that have been outdated by newer methods. For example, the <font> tag in standard HTML is now considered deprecated in favor of CSS font formatting.

**Element styles**

CSS styles that define the formatting of HTML elements, such as headings and paragraphs. An element style overrides any default formatting for an HTML element.

**External links**

Links to a page or resource outside a Web site.

**External style sheet**

An external text file that is saved with a .css extension and that contains style rules that define how various HTML elements display.

**Font set**

A set of three or more similar fonts that help ensure consistent text display in a variety of browsers and operating systems.

**GIF**

An image file format that can support a maximum of 256 colors. GIF files are best used for images with relatively few colors and with areas of flat color, such as line drawings, logos, and illustrations.

**HTML**

Hypertext Markup Language, the standard markup language on the Web. HTML consists of *tags* that define the basic structure of a Web page.

**ID styles**

Styles that allow you to create and name your own elements. While class styles can apply to multiple elements in a page, however, ID styles can be applied only to one element per page.

**Image map**

An image that contains multiple links called *hotspots*.

**Internal links**

Links to pages or resources within a Web site.

**Internal style sheet**

One or more style rules embedded in the head section of an HTML document. Styles in an internal style sheet can affect elements only in that document.

**Internet**

A vast array of networks that belong to universities, businesses, organizations, governments, and individuals all over the world.

**JPEG**

An image file format that supports more than 16 million colors. JPEG is best used for photographs and images that have many subtle color shadings.

**Link states**

The four states, or conditions that a link can be in: link, hover, active, and visited.

**Margin**

The space between page content and the edge of the browser window, or the space between individual elements.

**Monospaced font**

A typeface in which every character uses the same amount of space. For example, an "i" and an "m" take up the same amount of space on a line. Monospaced fonts, such as Courier, resemble typewriter text.

**Named anchor**

An element that you identify, by naming it, as an anchor, so you can link to it. Use the Named Anchor dialog box in Dreamweaver, or use the name attribute of the <a> tag, if you're working directly with code. Also called *bookmark links* or *intra-document links*, named anchors enable you to mark any spot on a page as a target and then link to that target.

**Nested list**

A list that's inside another list.

**Nested table**

A table that's inserted in the cell of another table.

**Non-breaking space**

A special HTML character that inserts a single space without breaking a line.

**Ordered list**

An HTML list structure that automatically appends sequential labels to each list item. By default, list items are numbered 1, 2, 3, and so on.

**Orphaned files**

Files that reside in your site folders but aren't linked to by any pages. These files might include early drafts of Web pages or image files that you decided not to use.

**PNG**

An image file format that combines some of the best features of JPEG and GIF. The PNG format supports more than 16 million colors and supports many levels of transparency. However, many older browsers don't fully support the PNG format.

**Sans-serif font**

A typeface whose characters don't have serifs (flourishes or ornaments at the ends of the strokes that make up the letters).

**Serif font**

A typeface whose characters have serifs (flourishes or ornaments at the ends of the strokes that make up the letters).

**Starter pages**

Page designs, included with Dreamweaver, that you can open and modify with your own content.

**Table cell**

The intersection of a row and column in a table. You insert content into table cells.

**Unordered list**

An HTML list structure that automatically appends bullets to each list item. Use this kind of list when the list items aren't sequential and don't need to be in any particular order.

**Visual Aids**

Page icons, symbols, or borders that are visible only within Dreamweaver. You can turn certain visual aids on and off to make it easier to work with the page.

**XHTML**

The Extensible Hypertext Markup Language is a strict version of HTML that doesn't allow proprietary tags and attributes, in favor of CSS control of all style information. XHTML allows for cleaner, more efficient code. By default, Dreamweaver CS3 builds Web pages with XHTML code.

# Index